Christmas 2007

Dear Chris,
Here's to Paris!
With love, Chloë x

PARIS
Contemporary Architecture

PARIS
Contemporary Architecture

Andrea Gleiniger
Gerhard Matzig
Sebastian Redecke

Prestel Munich · New York

Front cover: La Grande Arche, Johan Otto von Spreckelsen with Paul Andreu (Photo Felipe Ferré) (see pp. 28–31)
Back cover: Le Grand Louvre (Photo Stéphane Couturier) (see pp. 32–41) · Bibliothèque Nationale François Mitterrand (Photo Christian Richters) (see pp. 42–49) · Cité de la Musique (Photos Nicolas Borel) (see pp. 50–69) · Grand Stade Paris (see pp. 136–139)
Frontispiece: Drawing for the André Citroën Park by Patrick Berger (see pp. 116–125)

Library of Congress Cataloging-in-Publication Data is available.

Translated from the German by John Brownjohn
Editor: Peter Stepan
Copy-edited by Christopher Wynne

Prestel-Verlag
Mandlstrasse 26 · 80802 Munich, Germany
Tel. (+49–89) 38 17 09–0; Fax (+49–89) 38 17 09–35
and 16 West 22nd Street, New York, NY 10010, USA
Tel. (212) 627–8199; Fax (212) 627–9866

Prestel books are available worldwide. Please contact your nearest bookseller or write to either of the above addresses for information concerning your local distributor.

Designed by WIGEL, Munich
Lithography by Fischer Reprotechnik GmbH, Frankfurt am Main
Printed by Sellier Druck, Freising
Bound by R. Oldenbourg GmbH, Munich

Printed on acid-free paper
Printed in Germany

ISBN 3–7913–1655–9 (German edition)
ISBN 3–7913–1678–8 (English edition)

Contents

Foreword

If a nation's greatness is reflected in its buildings, France must indeed be the oft-invoked 'Grande Nation' – and not in European terms alone. In Versailles, France possesses the world's most imposing palace, and in the 'Grand Louvre' the largest museum, and in the Eiffel Tower the finest and loftiest monument to the art of civil engineering. Paris is a unique capital city, having for over 800 years been the undisputed hub of a country in which, as if under a gigantic magnifying glass, numerous buildings have risen during the last two decades to become resplendent examples of contemporary architecture whose very names bespeak their size and aspirations. Though fiercely criticized at first, the glass pyramid implanted beside Paris's palace of art by the architect Ieoh Ming Pei bears unmistakable testimony to the grandeur of the 'Grand Louvre' and is now, in close proximity to the city's most venerable architectural monuments, accepted as one of its major attractions. In the Tolbiac quarter, the soaring book-towers of Dominique Perrault's national library near the Gare d'Austerlitz, the Bibliothèque François Mitterrand, dominate the view across the Seine. This has been christened the 'TGB' – the 'très grande bibliothèque', or very big library, by analogy with France's celebrated prestige express train, the TGV. Johan Otto von Spreckelsen's monumental open cube in the La Défense district is – needless to say – entitled 'La Grande Arche', or Great Arch. Like an outsize picture-frame, this reinterpretation in stone of the Arc de Triomphe has focused people's gaze on a Paris of triumphal architectural superlatives and, with great self-assurance, created a gateway to the future of France. Not content with Garnier's old show-piece of an opera-house, the country has treated itself to an even bigger one in the Place de la Bastille. President François Mitterrand himself prescribed that this new 'people's opera', one of the few prestige projects in Paris that fails to carry urbanistic and architectural conviction, should be erected in that historic square.

In no other country and city in the world have large-scale, government-initiated buildings acquired such architectural and cultural importance as the 'Grands Projets de l'Etat' in Paris. It was inevitable that their sponsor, François Mitterrand, should be popularly elevated into 'Mitteramses'.

It is said that, in the last few years, some 90 per cent of the country's public works have been devoted solely to those Grands Projets whose bold architecture is now the talk of the world. Its conspicuous and imposing presence would seem to be mainly responsible for ensuring that the beauty on the Seine, hailed for centuries almost as an urban miracle, has, in our own time as well, become emblematically exalted into a grand prodigy of architectural muscle-flexing. Reason enough for a book like this – or so one might think. But are great buildings truly the foundation of architectural greatness? Isn't it also a fact that even the grammar of a grandiose city like Paris cannot, in the long run, dispense with architectural miniscules? What about all those relatively small buildings that likewise contribute to the great totality – 'lower case' buildings without which the 'capital letters' would make no sense in an urban context?

Any talk of contemporary architecture in Paris must also make mention of less ostentatious, less official specimens of exemplary architecture. Now is the very time, when the era of presidential Parisian architecture is coming to an end in the still unfinished Bibliothèque Nationale and people are increasingly readdressing themselves to questions of urban renewal, infilling, and housing shortages, in short, of social and aesthetic urban architecture; now, to repeat, is the very time to dedicate a book to those specimens of excellent architecture – shining examples but overshadowed by far more glamorous buildings – and to glean the qualitatively outstanding from the outwardly inconspicuous. Indeed, it is they, with their wondrous interplay of forms and materials, that have interested us in a special measure. That is why our architectural criticism devotes itself, not only to buildings already legendary for their magnitude, but also to those whose 'normality' skilfully asserts itself in contrast to the superlatives of scale; in other words, to those social housing developments, highway maintenance depots, office buildings, neighbourhood theatres, stadiums and post offices which sometimes, though not ennobled with the title 'grand', bear equal testimony to edifying architectural greatness.

Like the 'Grands Projets', they date in general from the present decade and its immediate predecessor. As in the case of their bigger fellows, our concern has been to exemplify rather than aim at documentary completeness. We did not wish our text and illustrations to present 'one-offs' alone, but, more particularly, infilling and ongoing construction projects of a sympathetic and restrained but self-assured nature. For it is probably this continuance of building, on both a large and a small scale, that renders Paris – more so, perhaps, than other cities – what it is and has been from time immemorial: a diverse and dynamic metropolis embodying the architectures of yesterday, today, and, doubtless, tomorrow as well.

The Authors

Building like God in Paris?

Gerhard Matzig

Paris is a ship – bellying sails, full speed ahead – with the following motto adorning its coat of arms: 'Fluctuat nec mergitur.' In other words, it tosses on the waves but doesn't sink. More than most cities, Paris tosses quite violently on the metropolitan sightseeing ocean, beset by billows of trippers, weekenders, cultural tourists, and travellers in luxury or on the cheap – lovers of Paris one and all. But it doesn't sink, thank goodness, not even in the storm of Parisian clichés, nor in the deluge of declarations of love sandwiched between the covers of novels, nor in the tempest of guidebooks, portraits, and pictorial volumes. It is almost a minor miracle that the city has not foundered under the weight of all the passions it has aroused throughout cultural history. In 1826 Heinrich Heine declared that he perceived in Paris 'a light so roseate that it brightens all tragedies'. Prince Hermann von Pückler-Müskau described Paris simply as 'the capital of the world', Chopin as 'paradise' and 'all you desire', and Ernest Hemingway as one long party. A heavenly world capital bathed in cheerful, rosy light – who would wish to improve on that?

What tribute to the beauty of Paris remains unspoken, what lover's vow has yet to be uttered? One cannot aspire to originality even when cursing the place, because angry outbursts have already occurred in very distinguished circles. Guy de Maupassant, for example, is credited with the following tirade: 'I quit Paris – France too, indeed – because the Eiffel Tower got on my nerves overmuch as time went by. I wonder what people will think of our generation if that tall, gaunt pyramid of metal ladders isn't soon torn down during an insurrection of some kind....' Hasn't everything long ago been said and written about the city of cities? One sometimes feels that the whole of cultural history could be studied by leafing through publications on Paris. Isn't that Proust, peering out in search of time past from between Notre-Dame, the Champs-Elysées and the Arc de Triomphe, the Dôme des Invalides and the Eiffel Tower, Sacré-Cœur and the Pont-Neuf? And there, that sounds like Piaf! Sartre is there, and so is de Beauvoir. Oscar Wilde, too, who on 10 October 1900, in the Hôtel d'Alsace, wrote: 'I am dying beyond my means.' They are all present: Gertrude Stein, Picasso, Saint-Exupéry, Fitzgerald, Truffaut, Montand, Hugo, Balzac – present, yet past. The Paris we know is culture turned to stone, but, above all, a kind of whispering imperfect tense. The past... history....

But those who now roam the alleyways and saunter along the boulevards of Paris, explore the parks and follow the Seine on its meanderings through the city, will discover stories of today amid the splendid scenery of the past. They will also find, away from the time-honoured sights, new things that are equally well worth seeing: interesting buildings, marvellous architecture, the Paris of today rather than yesterday. For it is, as ever, buildings that recount the stories of our time. And no other city, especially when one gets away from the 'Grands Projets', possesses buildings that so eloquently narrate in the present and future tenses and are so capable of bringing the present, too, to life in the mind's eye. Paris is neither London nor Berlin, Madrid nor Vienna, Hong Kong nor New York: architecturally speaking, it is the most fascinating and complex city of the present day, the national capital with the greatest and most varied wealth of contemporary buildings. A rosy light? Well, yes.

A German architectural theorist has proclaimed Paris, doubtless with good reason, 'the architectural metropolis'. Architects throughout the world clamour 'to learn' from Paris. Glossy magazines have long been unable to dispense with Parisian buildings, but professional publications, too, have wonderful things to report. Paris, the well-groomed model child of the architectural debate, or a simplistic stereotype of current architectural thinking? Has contemporary Parisian architecture itself already become one more myth in a city of myths, invented by those whose nostalgia for Paris illuminates the quest for a lost architectural culture? Is Paris the unreal figment of a dream, part of the delusion created by an illustrious architectural past and the skilful, effective marketing of a few comparatively successful public buildings? Yes and no, because Paris is meat for the devotee and the disparager alike. As Julien Green once asked the Parisians: 'What young architect will at last give us the city of the future, a handsome city whose effect on the coming generation will be as seductive as the way in which the Paris that gradually arose over the centuries contrived to enchant us? Is it too much to dream of a visionary that would be a poet of space...?'

In many places it is too much, and in many others one cannot be absolutely sure that the future is present and the poetry really there. In Paris, far from all that glitters so promisingly is gold. Glitter it does, though, and few can resist the city's uniquely exciting, wonderfully dynamic enthusiasm for architecture. One can almost reach out and grasp that which elsewhere finds its way into museums: architectural culture. Daily experience of building in the here and now, a knowledge of what is technically feasible, aesthetic experimentation and the arguments and wrangling that accompany it – such are the attributes that make Paris what it primarily is: vital and complex, with deep abysses and scintillating surfaces. In motion, too, so truly like a ship afloat on the river.

This is not self-evident, nor is it to history's credit, because modernity is only a rare constituent of the city's historical heritage. Quite unlike other European countries – Germany, for instance, or Austria, Holland, and Switzerland – France in general and her capital in particular were very wary of accepting our century's 'Neues Bauen'. There were Le Corbusier and his entourage, of course, but they were more of an élite exception to the general rule. So France, the very country where François Hennebique had signally pioneered the development of reinforced concrete in the 19th century, adhered for a surprising length of time to what may safely be termed 'classicism in ferroconcrete'. Moreover, France and Paris were slow to share the enthusiasm for the international character of the Modern Movement. Indeed, one critic advocated, to loud applause, that the French should go their 'own, national way'.

Finally, the trouble that most European countries had, and still have, with postwar modernists is not only well-known but, in Paris, notorious. 'Paris,' states a report on the city's condition in the early 1970s, 'had endured years of urbanistic terrorism.' This is a reference to the speculative razing of whole districts, the megacity concept, radical utopias (e.g. Yona Friedman's 'Paris spatial' or Paul Maymont's 'La traversée Paris'), and drastic encroachments everywhere. The results: Quai de Grenelle, La Défense, Quartier Italie, the demolition of Les Halles, the Tour Montparnasse. In the end, however, when public funds had ebbed and the flood of investors receded, Paris enjoyed a few years of cautious inquiry and respite from planning. This is what its architecture subsists on today. For the city's range of traditional retrospection, radical innovation and tentative progression seems to have generated a mixture of courage and defiance that has, in the past ten or twenty years, produced an almost incomparable diversity of architecture.

And here one should mention the many small but important advances in town planning; of the 'younger' generation of architects that has grown up in a climate characterized by a new understanding of urbanism; of the circumspect but strategically shrewd and energetic measures adopted by urban planners; of respect shown for the existing fabric; of the encouragement given to youthful talent; of contacts forged between architects and their clients; of academic innovations; and of the former head of state who, invested with positively feudal authority, knew how to manipulate his architectural power in an effective and coldly calculating manner, thereby setting an ideal image-building machine in motion.

The whole is more than the sum of its parts, for Parisian architecture is this, too: unaffectedly popular. Even today, as a matter of course, newly erected buildings bear a sign that proclaims the builder's name. Where else is that customary? Kitsch-consumers beside the Seine can even acquire an appalling specimen of modern architecture in oils, complete with sunset. Instead of Versailles – good, no? *Paris Match* carries almost regular reports on Parisian star architects and those who aspire to be such. Well, why not? In Paris, views on architecture do not stand in awe of it but blithely make themselves at home in the streets. The Eiffel Tower's beauty or monstrosity gave rise to wondrous altercations in its day. That is why Christian de Portzamparc's Cité de la Musique will survive being attacked by the graffiti artist who demonstratively sprayed its entrance with the question: 'Is this true architecture?'

Such are the controversies that have made Paris what it is today: a modern, wide-awake, lively city rife with lapses and aberrations, talents and exploited or squandered opportunities. A city with a long history and vast problems – a beautiful city filled with architecture but offering little in the way of explanations.

'When I was a child,' writes Julien Green, 'I often wondered how it was possible for the simple name Paris to describe so many different things. So many streets and squares, so many gardens, houses, roofs, chimneys, and above it all the changeable, airy sky that crowns our city; and the more I pondered on this, the more astonishing I found it that such a big city could be accommodated in such a short name. I uttered the two syllables again and again, and ended by finding them very mysterious indeed, because I asked myself: Why do people call it that and not something else? I fancied that I would discover something if I repeated the name often enough, but all I discovered in the end was that Paris is called Paris.'

Paris — Architecture and Urban Development in the 20th Century

Andrea Gleiniger

The Louvre, Notre-Dame, the Palais-Royal – miniatures of architectural history, isolated treasures boldly framed by the Cartesian solid geometries of a radically new urban vision: in 1925, in a series of pen-and-ink drawings that only hint at their dramatic break with tradition and change of scale, Le Corbusier projected the ideas and visions of his 'Ville Contemporaine' on to the centre of Paris. Originally conceived in 1922 as an imaginary, theoretical design for a modern city of three million inhabitants, it was now, three years later, assuming the shape of a provocative utopia overlaid on the city itself: Le Corbusier's 'Plan Voisin' proposed to use part of the right bank of the Seine as its actual construction site. Between the Rond-Point des Champs-Elysées, the Gare de l'Est and the Boulevarde Sébastopol, the very area where the city's architectural sediment was at its densest, he implanted a three-dimensional grid consisting of axial roads, green spaces, and cruciform skyscrapers 200 metres high: the traditional city was to be effaced and replaced by a wholly functional and functionalized services centre in which architectural history would survive as a museumized relic. The sensational vision which Le Corbusier first presented to the public in the 'Esprit Nouveau' pavilion at the Exposition d'arts décoratives in 1925 owed its name to Automobiles Voisin, the French car manufacturer,[1] and was a play on the anagrammatical relationship between 'voisin' and 'vision'. For the time being, however, he failed in his attempt to integrate the ideas of his city of the future, whose title so programmatically advertises its contemporary nature, in the official Parisian planning debate.

Now, after seventy years, it is as if a memorial to the Plan Voisin has been erected in a fragment of space as bold as it is isolated. The Bibliothèque Nationale's four glass slabs, which Dominique Perrault has coolly placed on a rectangular, stepped base opposite Bercy on the left bank of the Seine (see page 42), may strike many as a bibliophilic supersign. But something else can be inferred from the abstract cipher of the four open book covers: just as this ensemble of crystalline rectangles is in startling contrast to the conventions of library construction, whose typological history had always been little concerned with external shape and all the more innovatively so with the interior (and this in Paris, where Henri Labrouste had opened up new realms of thought some 150 years earlier with the ambitious cast-iron structures of the Bibliothèque Saint-Geneviève and the Bibliothèque Nationale), so Perrault's prisms jut from the Parisian skyline with startling abruptness; for the French capital's compact horizontality has always – discounting the rather isolated conglomeration of La Défense – held out against the obsessive crystallization of a vertical, skyscraper city.

All differences notwithstanding, it is not too hard to picture the L-shaped volumes duplicated into a cross so as to conjure up, pars pro toto, a vision of what the Paris of the 'Plan Voisin' might have looked like. And if we envision ourselves in the garden courtyard of the new library, can we not feel what Le Corbusier commended to his readers' imagination in 1929? 'You will be beneath trees.... Hardly a sound. You will see no buildings. How so? Through the branches, through the delightful arabesque network of the leaves, you will glimpse, widely spaced against the sky, huge masses of crystal...crystal that scintillates at night like a piece of electrical wizardry.'[2]

The Paris of the 1920s, which the artistic avant-garde, in its exhibitions, studios and galleries, had chosen as the workshop, showplace and mecca of the Moderne, found it hard to meet the challenges of modern architecture. Firmly rooted in the traditions of the Ecole des Beaux-Arts, the city had already undergone its dramatic reconstruction and was still, dependent on the unprecedented modernization to which it had been subjected by Baron Georges-Eugène Haussmann, who was appointed prefect of the Seine in 1853 and remained in office for almost two decades. Paris, whose population had crossed the million mark in 1846, was during that time subjected to far-reaching changes in town planning and infrastructure. The modernization of streets, power supplies and sewerage and the extensive construction of town halls, government buildings, ministries, schools, markets, slaughterhouses, hospitals, prisons, barracks, railway stations, et cetera, had transformed Paris into a uniquely 'well-equipped city'[3] and the very epitome of an urban, civic metropolis. It was this reconstruction that very largely established the Parisian myth to which countless memorials

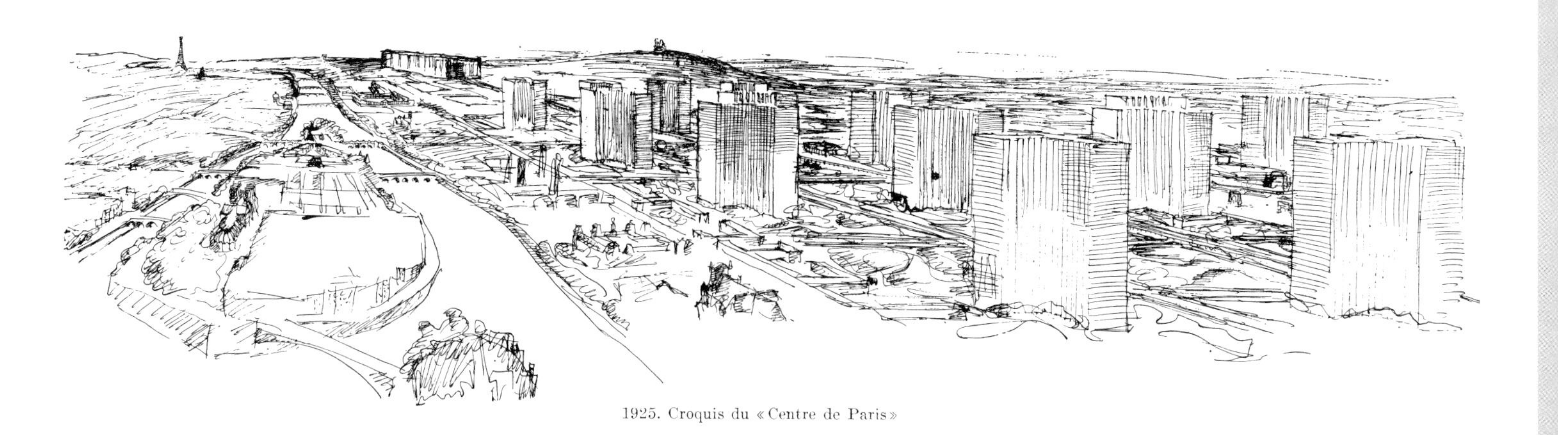

Le Corbusier's vision of a "ville contemporaine" in the centre of Paris, 1925

have been erected by writers and painters ranging from Emile Zola to Walter Benjamin and from Gustave Caillebotte to Auguste Renoir, Claude Monet, and Camille Pissarro. The city still subsists on this unique character, although it has been, and continues to be, exposed to increasingly radical visions of reconstruction and more rigid urbanistic measures since the Second World War.

Early improvements to the street network and the large-scale, 'ironed-out' block structures that sought to control and conceal the problem of mass housing behind impressive façades – a problem increasingly exported to the city's outskirts – gave promise of an urban system that would be equal to the challenges of the coming 20th century, at least within the area bounded by the ramparts of 1841, which underlay Haussmann's plans. Many old quarters in the west of the city fell prey to the blessings bestowed on it by the baron, but outside this hygienically reconstructed area, and especially in the east, there remained untouched whole districts that did more than breathe life into the sociological scenery of Honoré de Balzac or the mysterious melodramas of Eugène Sue. In their crowded destitution, the poor had re-formed and proliferated in new slums subject to the merciless dominion of speculators and landlords. Mass housing, which assumed the form of 'cités ouvrières'[4] in the underprivileged parts of Paris, played only a very minor role in Haussmann's urbanistic considerations, and, if it really stood in the way of his plans, was coldly and deliberately camouflaged by the façades of his new blocks. Left to the arbitrary calculations of landowners, mass housing developments in Paris generated the same squalor as in London or Berlin until, towards the end of the century, the efforts of housing reformers made themselves felt and the aegis of civic obligation was extended by rudimentary philanthropic ventures and subsidized housing programmes such as the 'Office des habitations à bon marché'. But little room remained in inner-city areas dominated by monuments, avenues, squares, boulevards, public buildings, and imposing residential blocks. The pressure released itself in the suburbs on the city's periphery, whose uncontrolled and oppressive growth became the chief impediment and problem of those who had inherited the baron's mantle and were striving, from the turn of the century onwards, to evolve overall plans and comprehensive regional development schemes.

Paris, too, proved a major challenge to town planning's evolution into a discipline in its own right, which had begun during the last decade of the 19th century with the aim of scientifically defining and professionally solving the complex problems of modern urban development. At the same time, late 19th-century Paris presented a glittering and contradictory picture in which technological innovation and academic tradition confronted each other in monuments of advanced engineering and spectacularly historicising exercises in style, both locked in a fierce struggle to produce the only valid concept of architecture.

It was, first and foremost, the regular succession of world exhibitions, often held in Paris between 1855 and 1937 and interrupted only once by the First World War, that presented a challenge to open up new areas or renovate and develop what already existed: the original Trocadéro, whose 'bizarre turquerie' was overlaid by the monumental classicism of the new Trocadéro in 1937, went up in 1878; 1889 witnessed displays of civil engineering such as the Eiffel Tower and the Galerie des Machines, subsequently demolished; and 1900 spawned the Grand and the Petit Palais. With the institutionalisation of town-planning bodies and committees under the pressure of urban growth, the first prerequisites for larger-scale competitions were in place.

The metropolitan reconstruction and development plans that took shape from the beginning of the century, at least on paper, did not pose any fundamental challenge to

Gustave Eiffel, Galerie des Machines, World Exhibition, Paris, 1889

Haussmann's principles. Those largely responsible for them were civil engineers whose main interest lay in transportation, and who came to regard the city primarily as a technological organism, a gigantic traffic and utility machine that concealed its 'true' character beneath the stylistic garb of historicism.

However much they differed on points of detail, men like Eugène Hénard, Jean-Claude-Nicolas Forestier, Louis Bonnier and Léon Jaussely adopted a general approach to the city that had two features in common: control of the periphery and optimization of the entire infrastructure. Hénard, in particular, made traffic the focal point of his deliberations and predicted a dominant role for the motor car. In his 'Etudes sur les transformations de Paris', published at regular intervals between 1903 and 1906, Hénard evolved some preliminary ideas for an automobile-friendly reconstruction of the city's historic heart and recommended drastic 'surgical' operations on its dense urban fabric. His 'Grande Croisée de Paris' scheme, which originated in 1904, proposed that Rue de Richelieu be extended into a north-south axis and that Rue Rambuteau, approaching it at right angles from the east, be extended in a westerly direction. The new thoroughfare would not only have done away with the area round the Palais-Royal, with its maze of narrow streets and sequestered alleyways; it would have cut through the Palais-Royal itself.[5] Although Hénard's studies were never put into effect, they had an undoubted influence, especially on the next generation. Le Corbusier, in particular, took up Hénard's ideas and radicalized them. In 1925 he located the east-west axis of his 'Plan Voisin' only a few hundred metres further north, near the Opéra, and years later he wanted this road to be construed as an alternative to the 'Route Triomphe', which, after being fiercely debated from 1906 onwards and again in the late 1920s, was largely completed after Second World War. A prolongation of the Champs-Elysées, this cut through the west of Paris to the disadvantage of the neglected urban districts in the east. Its final, monumental touches were imparted by the skyscraper platform of La Défense and Johann von Spreckelsen's Grande Arche, completed in 1989.

Hénard's studies had also evolved a modern type of thoroughfare that questioned the merits of the 'corridor street' tradition perfected by Haussmann and fiercely combated in later years by Le Corbusier. Hénard favoured looser alignments of buildings set further back and interspersed with green spaces. In his proposed 'rue à étages' the various types of traffic and utility systems were no longer laid out horizontally but vertically disposed on four levels and functionally divorced. The vision of a multi-storey traffic system, which had first been realized by the construction of the Métro, was also reflected in Louis Bonnier's proposal for a wide boulevard between whose elaborate façades traffic would circulate on a lower level while people idled, promenaded, and played games on the upper.

Hénard had some sympathy for the ideas of Ebenezer Howard, whose garden city concept, based on the example of Greater London, was creating a sensation on the Continent. Where Paris was concerned, however, Hénard proposed to condense its existing residential quarters still further, supplementing them with some loose-knit housing developments and a series of parks running along the old fortifications. Forestier pursued this line of Hénard's in 1906, when he recommended an extensive system of parks encircling Paris.

It is clear that the Paris planning authorities were little influenced in their deliberations by the ideas and visions of new, rationally planned housing developments and entire urban districts like those formulated by Howard in his 'garden cities' and by Toni Garnier in his plans for a 'cité industrielle', which he evolved from 1900 onwards. In 1913, when Louis Bonnier and the historian Marcel Poëte presented the recently established committee for urban expansion with a comprehensive project predominantly concerned with the technological requirements of urban development, they also recommended the construction of two garden cities, one each in the north and south. It was not until the late 1920s, after the interruption occasioned by the First World War, that the first garden city-like plans took shape and the architectonic developments exemplified by the 'Neues Bauen' housing that had since gone up in Holland and Germany were adopted in the 'Butte Rouge' development at Chatenay-Malabry.

Bonnier's and Poëte's deliberations of 1913 did, however, pave the way for a town-planning competition advertised after the First World War. It was won by Léon Jaussely, who defined the whole of Paris as a unitary economic organism whose functional efficiency was dependent on the efficiency and practical layout of its infrastructure of canals, railway lines, and streets.[6]

Otherwise than in Vienna, Berlin, Frankfurt, Amsterdam or Rotterdam, where subsidized housing had been identified as a civic duty and become a field for experiments by the architectural avant-garde, French housing development plans remained architecturally traditional. From 1919 onwards, under the aegis of the 'Office des habitations à bon marché', a series of subsidized housing developments grew up along the line of old fortifications demolished after the First World War: dense, compact urban developments which, although they loosened and opened up the Parisian block system, retained their commitment to a conservative repertoire of designs until the 1930s.

Among the most notable inner-city projects were the terraced dwellings designed by Henri Sauvage, who had been developing the terraced mode of construction since 1909. In 1912, financed by an association founded expressly for the purpose by his friends, the 'Société des Maisons à Gradins', Sauvage erected a first example of this type of building in Rue Vavin, not far from the Jardins du Luxembourg.[7] Created for a rather exclusive clientele drawn from the artistic and intellectual avant-garde, Sauvage's development was a prototypal demonstration of his ideas on hygienic, healthy housing with good access to air and sunlight. The stepped façade, which provided each apartment with a terrace from the second storey up, looked unusual enough in itself in the conventional setting of a Parisian street. But Sauvage had faced the whole building with white tiles whose gleaming uniformity was accentuated only by the shadows cast by the function-dictated profile of the façade and the very sparing use of a geometrical ornament composed of dark blue tiles. The glazed tiles' clinical character underscored the hygienic pretensions of an architecture that Sauvage wished to be construed as a manifesto against the inhuman and unhealthy conditions prevailing in inner-city apartment houses infested with tuberculosis. He was not long afterwards granted an opportunity, under the auspices of 'Habitations à bon marché', to erect a block of flats for workers in the north of the city. Between 1916 and 1926 there arose, in the bend of Rue des Amiraux, a complex terraced on all sides and faced with white ceramic tiles. Its aspirations in the field of public health are additionally documented and validated by a multipurpose hall and, more particularly, by the indoor swimming pool in the centre of the complex, which is still in public use today.

Sauvage received few commissions for sizeable public buildings and is still overshadowed by his far more celebrated (academician) colleagues Perret and Garnier on the one hand,

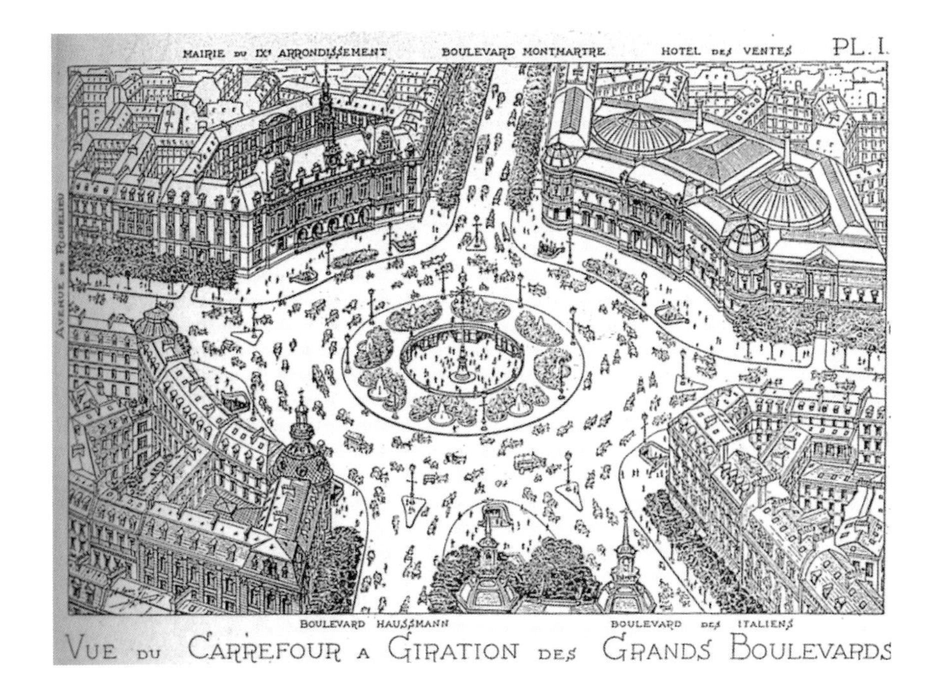

Eugène Hénard, roundabout at junction of the boulevards, from 'Etudes sur les transformations de Paris', 1906

Louis Bonnier, project for a boulevard on two levels

Henri Sauvage, apartment block with stepped façade and terraces in the Rue Vavin, Paris, 1912

Alexandre Maistrasse, the "garden city" at Suresnes, 1921–39

and, on the other, by prominent exponents of 'nouvelle architecture' on the other. What he executed in miniature in these apartment houses acquired a monumental, Futurist-inspired impact in his town-planning schemes: twenty-odd storeys high, his terraced, monolithic blocks resemble ziggurats. Even in 1931, or shortly before his death, he designed two terraced, pyramidal buildings pierced by angular entrance towers for the gatelike development of Porte Maillot: a response to the Arc de Triomphe at the other end of the axis.[8]

The development of the Parisian suburbs remained one of the biggest problems the city had to contend with. Residential districts there tended to be conventional in their architectural layout and social pretensions, and are not to be compared with the housing developments that originated in Germany and Holland from the early 1920s onwards. That was when the first large-scale, 'rural' housing developments at Suresnes, Lilas and Genevilliers were initiated by the Office Public d'Habitation under the direction of Henri Selliers.[9] It was not, however, until the garden city of Butte Rouge arose that French housing developments achieved a link-up with those elsewhere in Europe. Built between 1929 and 1934, Butte Rouge was designed by the architects Joseph Massompierre, Paul Ruffé and Paul Sirvin, who had put forward a comprehensive garden city project for Paris in 1919.[10] Spatially complex and multiform, Chatenay-Malabry owes much of its inspiration to Ernst May's housing developments at Frankfurt and the Dutch domestic architecture designed by Jakobus Johannes Pieter Oud. At a time when the original wealth of design characteristic of modern housing developments was being subjected to ever more rigid rationalization and economic and political constraints, particularly in Germany, there arose in the garden city of Butte Rouge, with its responsiveness to symmetries

and axes, a kind of iconographic extract of what German and Dutch housing developments had produced in the way of spatial and architectonic variety.

'The Académie has breached the Boulevard Haussmann. It is planning to construct Paris's "route triomphale", which will end at the Etoile. It requires honours and trophies; it insists on fancying itself present at Caesar's triumph. It forgets that Paris is dying of anaemia, crushed by the machine. Triumphs and festive processions are in preparation for this city beset by dangers.... But the city will be destroyed by tuberculosis, commerce by congestion, and the countryside by paralysis. What does the Académie care? It will have its trophies.' (Le Corbusier, 1929.)

On his arrival in Paris in 1908, Le Corbusier took Eugène Grasset's advice and joined the studio of Auguste Perret, who had been running it since 1905 with his brother, the building contractor Gustave Perret. Born in 1874, Auguste Perret had successfully attended the Ecole des Beaux-Arts without actually completing the course. At this stage in the brief history of ferroconcrete construction, he had already caused something of a stir by designing three 'epoch-making buildings':[11] the casino at Saint-Malo (1899), the apartment house in Rue Franklin (1903), and the four-storeyed garage in Rue de Ponthieu (1905). Perret regarded ferroconcrete as 'the perfectly homogeneous system' he required in order to achieve the synthesis of the classical (i.e. Greek) and Gothic ideals whose conflict had so greatly exercised the Ecole des Beaux-Arts.[12] The innovative feature of the Rue Franklin apartment house consists not only in a load-bearing structure of concrete supports, which afforded Perret greater scope for ground-plan solutions, but also in the clear differentiation between structural elements and cladding. Although the concrete is nowhere visible, being entirely faced with ceramic tiles, the difference is articulated by the use of ornamented and monochrome tiles. However, Perret's interest in the innovative potentialities of new building systems and their spatial and formal effects was always at the service of an architectural language that invoked the traditional – classical – formal canon and submitted it to rational revision.

It was this that ultimately brought him, the moderate innovator in the orbit of the Académie, into violent conflict with the budding avant-garde, notably Le Corbusier, whose 1922 pamphlet 'Vers une architecture' caused Perret to engage in fierce polemics. Their target, who had praised and defended Perret's Rue Franklin apartment house as a manifesto on the road to a 'nouvelle architecture',[13] remained largely unmoved: 'Perret is no revolutionary; he perpetuates the great, noble, elegant truths of French architecture.'[14]

In the same year as Le Corbusier's 'Ville Contemporaine' appeared, Perret likewise advanced an ideal metropolitan development scheme for 'le bon vieux Paris'. So as to avoid inflicting undue damage on historic Paris, Perret projected his 'Avenue de Maisons Tours' onto the former ring of fortifications. Articulated with outsize columns and pilasters and linked by gigantic arches, some 100 of his austerely designed skyscrapers, each 150 to 200 metres high and accomodating as many as 3000 people, were to flank a wide boulevard interspersed with green spaces. Unlike Le Corbusier's, Perret's towers were intended to contain living accommodation, not offices. It is, perhaps, significant that Le Corbusier, whose own scheme could not have been more radical, criticized Perret's design for being monumental and classicistic, accusing him of having exceeded the bounds of reason and cast a dangerously Futuristic shadow over what was, in essence, a sound idea.[15]

The architectural innovations of the first third of the 20th century can be detected at many points in Paris, even though the city has assimilated most of them in its own very characteristic way. They often lead an entirely secluded existence, for unlike those of the 19th century they have retained their structure unchanged, or almost so. Not only Perret's or Sauvage's buildings, or the few executed in Paris by Garnier, or the examples of Art Nouveau, which represents a comparatively brief intermezzo in Parisian façade and road

Joseph Bassompierre, Paul de Ruffé and Paul Sirvin, the "garden city" at Butte-Rouge, Chatenay-Malabry, 1929–34

Auguste Perret, proposal for an "Avenue des Maison-Tours" followng the line of Paris' historic defenses, 1922

Auguste Perret, apartment block in Rue Franklin, Paris, 1903

construction, but also the 'Neues Bauen' specimens that won lasting fame as isolated incunabula in the history of modern architecture – the city has here and there, after turbulent interludes, assimilated all these styles and transformed them into a rather incidental occurrence, a marginal note in its architectural history.

The house at the foot of Montmartre built in 1926 for the Dadaist Tristan Tzara by Adolf Loos, who had been resident in Paris since 1922, is his most important building of the 1920s and constitutes a summary of his architectonic principles: the tall, bare, rectangular façade, which almost defiantly confronts its surroundings, is divided into two. The two-storeyed base of exposed stone is surmounted by a pale expanse of cladding of the same height. Neither ornaments nor 'handsome volumes' articulate the symmetrical façade, which is structured only by sharply incised window embrasures and loggialike recesses. The materials are commonplace, but their mode of use creates a drastic contrast that underscores the architecture's uncompromising character.

Loos was not alone in building for an artist in Paris. The clientele of the architectural avant-garde was drawn almost entirely from artistic and intellectual circles. Other than in Germany or Holland, where, over and above the spectacular buildings and architectural manifestos produced by the construction of villas and exclusive one-family dwellings, official housing policy and 'Neues Bauen' made common cause for a brief but highly productive period, and other than in Italy, where modern architecture became official policy, at least for a certain length of time, it was mainly private individuals who espoused the novel architectural ideas disseminated not least by *L'Esprit nouveau*, the periodical launched by Le Corbusier in 1919. They commissioned villas, houses and studios that were acclaimed as more than unique events, e.g. the house for Amedée Ozenfant (1923) situated near some small, picturesque suburban houses near of Montsouris reservoir (in 1927, only a few years later, André Lurçat built the Villa Guggenbuhl not far away); in the course of the 1920s a handful of small artists' colonies arose which, like microcosms of the avant-garde, bore witness to the new

architecture. Le Corbusier, too, had it in mind to build a complex of several houses when looking for a suitable site in Paris in 1923 (the year the De Stijl exhibition was held there). Vigorously wheeling and dealing, Le Corbusier 'spent a great deal of time visiting building sites all over Paris with a view to offering them to his clients, many of whom were in some way associated with the periodical *L'Esprit nouveau*, as a package, i.e. house and site in one.'[16] He almost succeeded in developing a small street in its entirety, namely, the cul-de-sac leading to the Place du Docteur Blanche. Of the four houses originally intended to occupy these sites as parts of a single scheme, two were eventually built between 1923 and 1925: one for the banker and art collector Raoul La Roche, and the other for the architect's brother-in-law and partner Pierre Jeanneret and his Swedish wife Lotti Rääf (now the Fondation Corbusier).

In the villa for La Roche, whose collection of modern art became a factor vital to its architectonic design, Le Corbusier made his first programmatic use of piles, strip windows, a ramp, and roof garden as basic elements typical of his vocabulary. He staged what he termed a 'promenade architecturale': as one walked through the house, the 'spectacle architectural' was intended to manifest itself as a striking composition made up of diverse visual angles and surprising perspectives, lighting and colour effects.[17] Together with his many smaller villas and houses in and around Paris, the Villa La Roche, the Villa Stein at Garches and the Villa Savoie are not only Le Corbusier's most important specimens of domestic architecture but incunabula of the Moderne itself. Unlike his Salvation Army headquarters, which went up between 1929 and 1931 and retains its original function to this day, they are cloaked in an aura of exclusivity.

Not long afterwards, Lurçat and Robert Mallet-Stevens were able to realize Le Corbusier's aim of designing a small street in its entirety. An artists' colony and 'architectural exhibition' combined, this – unusually enough – embodies urban (inner-city) forms of development that display compactness and uniformity. The eight studio dwellings comprising the Villa Seurat (in Rue de la Tombe-Issoire, a cul-de-sac near the Parc de Montsouris) originated in 1925–6. Discounting the studio for the Russian sculptress Chana Orloff, which is Perret's work, it was Lurçat who designed these houses for a clientele of painters and writers, among them his brother Jean. The density of the surrounding built-up area prompted the architects to adopt a rather introverted format whose spatial complexity and variety unfolds mainly within, behind the 'façade'. Lurçat consistently adhered to a Purist, De Stijl-inspired formal language that accords each house its individuality but acquires a great unity of design in which decorative effects and the structure of Perret's architecture become contrapuntal. By developing the Cité Seurat, Lurçat gained a leading position among exponents of the 'nouvelle architecture' that was not, for the time being, in any way inferior to Le Corbusier's.

The Cité Seurat set a pattern for Rue Mallet-Stevens. Barely a hundred metres from the present Fondation Corbusier, this was developed one year later by Mallet-Stevens, who not only succeeded in acquiring a far wealthier clientele for his project but contrived to immortalize himself during his lifetime in the name of the street (another cul-de-sac). Mallet-Stevens was the member of the triumvirate at the head of the 'nouvelle architecture' who cared least, or not at all, about the social and socio-political implications of modern architecture. He, who devoted the whole of his rather brief career to building luxury villas and houses, employed this rare opportunity to design an entire street-space mainly to demonstrate his conception of architectonic design, in which a central role was played by the sculptural conformation of volumes. Rendered in white, the stereometrically smooth volumes of his structural elements acquire their plastic rhythm from terracing and echeloning by means of towers and canopies, and from the way in which smooth, taut expanses of wall are relieved and articulated with window openings of varying shapes and dimensions.

Several of these houses have since been altered and one or two have disappeared. An architecture that has long ago, and in the most natural way, been assimilated by the urban landscape of Paris is often obscured by additional window embrasures and altered formats, displaced entrances, and a variety of annexes and extensions. Now that they have grown into the existing fabric, we can only vaguely imagine how provocative the rectangles and cubes of 'nouvelle architecture' must have looked in a city whose architecture was largely determined by representatives of the Ecole des Beaux-Arts. Only in very recent times have writers on architectural history elicited and reminded us that a far more exciting and innovative range of architectonic solutions had begun to take shape, even in their ranks, than we are encouraged to believe by the modern, generalized view of the eclecticism and formal traditionalism of buildings dating from after the turn of the century – a view greatly fostered by Le Corbusier's polemics.

Town planning in the 1920s and 1930s was largely the preserve of technocratic civil engineers, whereas the ideas of the Moderne did not permeate architecture – albeit briefly – until the end of the 1920s. That was when, in addition to villas and artists' colonies, there came into being public or official buildings such as the Salvation Army headquarters (1929–31) in the 13th Arrondissement and the Swiss Pavilion (1932) in the Cité Universitaire, amid whose green spaces and heterogeneous architectural landscape Le Corbusier's building – quite unlike the Brazilian Pavilion he designed in collaboration with Costa during the 1950s – represents a

Robert Mallet-Stevens, corner house, part of the project in Rue Mallet-Stevens, Paris, 1927

veritable gem. But building activity in France, too, was badly affected by the consequences of the Depression. One major victim was the programme set forth in 1928 by Louis Loucher, the minister of labour, who had sponsored a law for the state subvention of affordable housing. Probably the most spectacular and trail-blazing result of this policy, apart from the aforementioned garden city of Butte Rouge at Chatenay-Malabry, is the La Muette development at Draincy designed by Marcel Lods and Eugène Beaudouin (1931–4). Here, the architects had combined two different types of buildings on a linear, rational ground-plan: the more modest, 'à bon marché' dwellings are accommodated in high-rise blocks of sixteen storeys, while those of better quality, classified as 'à bon marché amélioré', are in blocks of three and four storeys.[18] With their open-air school in Suresnes (1935) and their Maison du Peuple in Clichy, which demonstrates a 'bold handling of functionalism and technology'[19] and was finally completed in 1939 in collaboration with Jean Prouvé and Wladimir Bodanski, Lods and Beaudouin were among the few architects who remained true to the principles of the Moderne. Their 1934 design for an exhibition centre at La Défense was never realized. The bold dynamics of a double steel spiral distantly related to Tatlin's monument to the Third International, together with a roof structure of steel cables reminiscent of wheel spokes, render the design a monumental allegory of speed and space-pervading motion.

By 1937, when Paris once more staged a presentation of 'the spirit of the age', the architectural scene had changed dramatically. In line with the 'neo-humanism' that had been gaining ground since the early 1930s, the demand for a 'national tradition' in architecture, alias a conception of it that invoked the country's classicistic heritage, was also in the ascendant.[20] The buildings on show at the 'Exposition Internationale des Arts et Technique', the sixth international exhibition to be held in Paris, were primarily demonstrative of a heroic, monumental style that paid homage to a vague species of classicism, a distillation of set pieces drawn from all parts of the ancient world and all its historical adaptations. It was on the occasion of this world exhibition, at which the Third Reich grandly paraded itself before the outside world through the medium of Albert Speer's German Pavilion, that the Musée d'Art Moderne originated after a classicistic, academic design by Jean-Claude Dondel, A. Aubert, P. Viard, and M. Dastugue. Over the remains of the Trocadéro, built in 1878 and partly demolished, Léon Azéma, Louis-Hippolyte Boileau and Jacques Carlu erected the Palais de Chaillot, whose 'lingering, attenuated classicism' was intended less to produce 'an exact repetition of the traditional canon of design than to invoke a French tradition of monumental spatial axes'[21] and express national emotion. The design of the new Trocadéro, which overlays the semicircle of the old with a range of monumental columns and adorns it with the bombastic archways that rise above the immense terrace, underlined and monumentalized its spatial relationship to the Eiffel Tower across the Seine, the Champs de Mars beyond, and, in the east, the domed Ecole Militaire. The pretensions of this axis were accentuated by the angular, heroic stereometry of the Soviet Pavilion and the arrogant bombast of the German.

Little remained amid this spatial setting's totalitarian rationality and cold academicism of the modernity whose presence was largely confined to Le Corbusier's urbanistic schemes ('Ville Radieuse'), which were also on display. Even the enlightened academicism of Perret, who had submitted a very promising and highly regarded design for the Palais de Chaillot in 1933, found no place in this renewed revival of French (architectural) tradition, which aspired to be construed primarily as a vague reversion to the architecture of the 18th century and apodictically demanded the formal allegiance of the moderns.

One of the last examples of explicitly modern and technologically oriented architecture within the precincts of

the French capital was the Maison du Peuple in Clichy, completed before the Second World War and the German occupation brought building activity to an end.

In 1939 the government finally approved an overall plan for the urban development of Paris. This had been initiated a good decade earlier by the 'Comité supérieur de l'aménagement de la Région parisienne', established in 1928. Raoul Dautry, an engineer and senior executive with the French railway companies, and Henri Prost, a town planner and architect noted for his work at Anvers (1910) and in Morocco, had laid the foundations of a concentrated process of urban development in the Paris region centred on Notre-Dame and covering an area seven kilometres in diameter. The avowed aim of this scheme was to check unsystematic overspill on the city's outskirts and to regulate and supervise expansion in accordance with an overriding technological and organizational plan.[22]

Le Corbusier's 'Plan Voisin' had been the earliest and most provocative in a whole series of attempts, extending into the 1940s, to intervene in the Parisian planning debate and drive a modernist wedge into the city's traditional fabric. His visionary assault on its historic centre was succeeded by smaller-scale proposals that addressed the depressing actuality of those 'quartiers insalubres', especially in the east of Paris, where inner-city living conditions had dramatically deteriorated. The projects he submitted in 1937 had, for instance, included a plan for the radical reconstruction of 'Ilot no. 6',[23] an exceptionally deprived area in the 12th Arrondissement. This was where Le Corbusier had proposed to implant one of his 'Ville radieuse' quarters, and he took advantage of this project to make detailed comparisons with the population density, land utilization, etc., of prevailing examples of official Parisian housing construction.[24] Although he again sought every opportunity to put his scheme into effect, it too remained a waste of paper. When the war ended he made one last, more detailed attempt to promote the reconstruction of the relatively undamaged city, but his proposals met with no success there. His first 'unité d'habitation' went up in Marseille, and his ideas on town planning eventually bore fruit in altogether different places.

A new plan for regional development and organization came into being in 1956. Its primary aim was to relieve the dense inner-city structure by creating focal points of population density in the inner suburbs.[25] Decentralization was the watchword, and its earliest manifestations were the transfer of the capital's covered markets to Rungis and the development of La Défense into a skyscraper citadel. This scheme was followed in the late 1950s by a series of urbanistic utopias that sought salvation not only in designs for entirely new towns but in spectacular urban visions in which Paris was to be overbuilt with huge tentlike structures and interminable, megalomaniac expanses of latticework. Whereas all previous urban utopias had been characterized by their contact with the ground, and whereas urbanists and planners still believed that they could master the manifold tasks and problems of urban development 'on the basis of the facts', visionaries like Yona Friedman broke with tradition altogether and aimed for the stars.

The 'Ville spatiale', whose flexible and neutral framework technology would, pursuant to Friedman's ideas, overlay existing Paris with a second urban system remote from the ground and composed of mobile capsules and prefabricated, serial supports and space frames, is a particularly vivid illustration of the technology-obsessed projections of the future that had to be abruptly reconsidered because of the oil crisis in the early 1970s. But, even though Friedman's plans were no more put into effect than those of all the other utopians, traces of them can be discerned in the gigantic housing developments that have so questionably taken shape on the outskirts of Paris since the 1960s. Although originally based in the main on socially defined concepts of space that sought to eliminate the problem of mass population by consigning it to abstract supersculptures, they became increasingly transmuted during the 1970s into formal arrangements that strove for plasticity. But the upright Camembert boxes of the 'Arènes de Picasso' were quite as incapable as Bofill's monumental construction set of compensating for the urbanistic and, consequently, social deficiencies of these mass agglomerations or of resolving the problem of the periphery.

Even though they detract little from the myth of 'the capital of the 19th century', the 1960s and 1970s are no glorious chapter in the history of Paris, either architecturally or urbanistically.[26] The utopias of the late 1950s may not have been realized, but they were depressingly echoed by the large-scale housing projects that sprang up mainly in eastern suburbs like Marne-la-Vallée or Evry, and by those wholesale redevelopments whose victims, though not confined to much-mourned treasures like Les Halles (1971) or the panopticon of La Roquette, included several square kilometres of historic urban fabric. The Tour Montparnasse put paid to a whole neighbourhood inhabited (and kept alive) by artists and craftsmen. The high-rise buildings erected along the Quai de Grenelle at the foot of the Eiffel Tower are primarily illustrative of the way in which postwar functionalism has been perverted. And what of La Défense?

The often hopeless condition of the 'quartiers insalubres' made wholesale demolition seem the only sensible answer, but the planners' recourse to such radical purges was far from motivated by the welfare-oriented, hygienic ethos of prewar modern architecture. In the 'radicalism of their rigid master plans'[27] the technocrats of the postwar period took

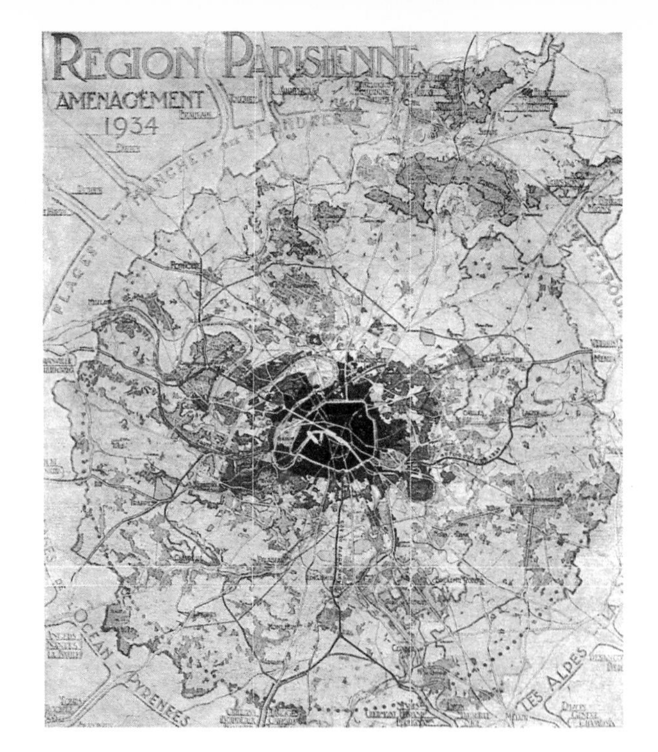

Henri Post, plan for urban development in the Paris region, 1934

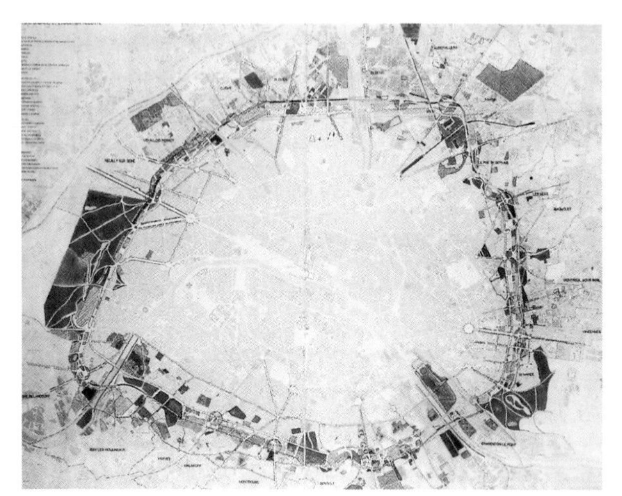

Atelier Parisien d'Urbanisme/Institut d'Aménagement et d'Urbanisme de la Région Ile de France, plan for suburban development, 1980s

over the urbanistic concepts of the Moderne and/or those of Le Corbusier in a thoroughly questionable manner. Architectural requirements fell by the wayside and all connection with the traditional city and its urban quality was destroyed by their megasculptural, bird's-eye-view planning exercises and their primarily abstract, sociologically defined spatial concepts.

Paris was, for a short time, rendered accessible to change. That which planners had often dreamed of since the beginning of the century seemed possible at last: a farewell to restrictions on height and the corridor street's continuous building lines and façades.[28] But the 'lyricism' so vehemently demanded by Le Corbusier, who thought it suited to 'grasping the rational idea and imparting it to the benefit of architecture',[29] was missing. On the contrary: 'Though spared by the war, Paris at the beginning of the 1970s is a partially mutilated city. It has undergone years of urbanistic terrorism.'[30]

But in France, too, the generation of women architects who had emerged and established themselves in early projects since the end of the 1970s began to seek impulses and guidelines pointing in a new direction. They rejected the building of more satellite towns[31] and were mindful of the complex fabric of the traditional city and its urban culture. But they did not simply renovate; they sought a fundamental reordering of urban and urbanistic morphology. The 'Atelier Parisien d'Urbanisme' (APUR) was founded back in 1967. At first a theoretically oriented syndicate opposed to official town-planning directives, APUR became in 1978 an official organ of the Paris planning authority.[32] From the beginning of the 1980s APUR evolved an extensive redevelopment programme centred mainly on individual buildings and ensembles, derelict industrial premises, run-down residential districts, et cetera, in the east of Paris. A multitude of new and redevelopment projects, the so-called ZAC (Zones d'aménagement concertées), are intended to sustain, restore and renew those attributes which, over and above its monumental buildings and 'Grands Projets', make a city what it is: plurality and urban vitality.

1 Unlike Citroën and Peugeot, the French automobile and aircraft manufacturer Gabriel Voisin (1880–1973) lent his name to Le Corbusier's plan for Paris and helped to finance his *L'Esprit nouveau* pavilion. See *Le Corbusier: une encyclopédie*, exhibition cat., Paris, 1987, p. 470.

2 *Le Corbusier et Pierre Jeanneret, Œuvre complet*, vol. 1, 1910–29, ed. by W. Boesiger and O. Stonorov, Zurich, 1991 (3rd ed.), p. 120.

3 Philippe Panerai, Jean Castex, and Jean-Charles Depaule, *Vom Block zur Zeile. Wandlungen der Stadtstruktur*, Braunschweig/Wiesbaden, 1985, p. 16.

4 See Gilles Barbey, *'WohnHaft'. Essay über die innere Geschichte der Massenwohnung*, Braunschweig/Wiesbaden, 1984, p. 22 ff.

5 Alain Guiheux, Eugène Hénard, and Toni Garnier, 'Le règne de la circulation', *La Ville, art et architecture en Europe 1870–1993*, ed. by Jean Dethier and Alain Guiheux, Paris, 1994, pp. 153–7.

6 See Nicole Toutcheff, 'Léon Jaussely (1875–1932). Les débuts de l'urbanisme scientifique en France', ibid., pp. 169–71.

7 Jean-Baptiste Minaert, 'Henri Sauvage (1873–1932)', ibid., p. 198 f. On Sauvage's apartment house in Rue Vavin see Jean-Louis Cohen, Monique Eleb, and Antonio Martinelli, 'The 20th Century Architecture and Urbanism: Paris', *a & u*, 9/1990, Tokyo, 1990, pp. 50–8.

8 Ibid., p. 198.

9 Jean-Louis Cohen, 'Metropolis or the impossible plan', ibid., pp. 10–16; id., 'De la ville à la région: l'extension de Paris au XXe siècle', *Paris. La ville et ses projets*, exhibition cat., Paris, 1988, pp. 212–21.

10 *a & u*, 9/1990, 114–25.

11 See Kenneth Frampton, *Grundlagen der Architektur. Studien zur Kultur des Tektonischen*, Munich, 1993, p. 129 ff.

12 Ibid., p. 132.

13 *Le Corbusier et Pierre Jeanneret, Œuvre complet*, 1910–29, introduction to 1st ed., Zurich, 1964, p. 14. See also Roberto Gargiani, *Paris. Architektur zwischen Purismus und Beaux-Arts 1919–1939*, Braunschweig/Wiesbaden, 1992, p. 10.

14 From *Hervé Martin, Moderne Architektur Paris 1900–1995*, Berlin, undated, p. 205.

15 Joseph Abran, 'Auguste Perret et la ville', Paris 1994, p. 321.

16 Tim Benton, 'Raoul La Roche – Sammlung und Haus', *L'Esprit nouveau. Le Corbusier und die Industrie 1920–1925*, ed. by Stanislaus von Moos, Berlin, 1987, p. 82.

17 See Le Corbusier (v.n.13), 1964, p. 60.

18 Pieter Uyttenhove, 'La cité de la Muette à Draincy', Paris 1994, p. 325.

19 Jean-Louis Cohen, 'Architektonischer Rationalismus und Modernisierung in Europa zwischen den Weltkriegen' in *'Die Axt hat geblüht...', Europäische Konflikte der 30er Jahre in Erinnerung an die frühe Avantgarde*, ed. by Jürgen Harten, Hans-Werner Schmidt, and Marie Luise Syring, exhibition cat., Düsseldorf, 1987, p. 72.

20 See Richard Hüttel, 'Neo-Klassizismus oder Aneignung der nationalen Baugeschichte – Zur Architektur im Jahre 1937', ibid., p. 79 f.

21 Ibid., p. 80.

22 Nicole Toutcheff, *Henri Prost (1874–1959) Anvers, Casablanca, Paris*, Paris 1994, p. 172 f. See also Cohen, 1988 (v. n. 9).

23 Le Corbusier, 1988, p. 292 f.

24 Ibid., p. 293.

25 Cohen, 1988 (v.n.9), p. 242.

26 See Dominique Rouillard, 'Paris, point par point,' *Bauwelt*, 1/2, 1992, p. 14 ff.

27 Reinhart Wustlich, 'Neue Architektur in Frankreich. Abschied vom Über-Ich – Entwicklungen in der emanzipierten Provinz', Centrum, *Jahrbuch für Architektur und Städtebau*, ed. by Peter Neitzke and Carl Steckeweh, Braunschweig/Wiesbaden, 1994, p. 241.

28 Rouillard, 1992 (v.n.26), p. 14.

29 Le Corbusier (v.n.13), 1964, p. 120.

30 Wustlich, 1994 (v.n.27).

31 Ibid.

32 Marie-Jeanne Dumont, 'L'époque Apur vingt-cinq ans d'histoire', *L'Architecture d'Aujourd'hui*, 294/1994, p. 64 f.

France and François Mitterrand's 'Grands Projets'

Sebastian Redecke

In the capital of no other European country in recent decades have government-initiated, large-scale buildings, most of them open to the public, aroused such widespread interest in architecture and town planning but, at the same time, triggered such heated debates as the numerous 'Grands Projets de l'Etat' in Paris. The first four projects in this development so fundamental to the city's appearance had been inherited from his predecessors in 1981 by President François Mitterrand, who died in January 1996. He not only pursued them with great enthusiasm but raised them to a new dimension. More than that, the 'Grands Projets' became one of the most important tasks he performed during his long period in office. An extremely far-sighted man who had dedicated himself to a humane society supportive of national culture, he regarded those projects as harbingers of the next millennium and thus, of a new epoch.

Mitterrand was successful. He managed to accomplish nearly all his major plans for the capital. Having been spectacularly initiated under President Georges Pompidou with the planning of the Centre Beaubourg, the process ended with Mitterrand's gigantic scheme for a new, central Bibliothèque Nationale de France, which he was able to inaugurate a few weeks before quitting the political stage. Jacques Chirac, the new President, has yet to announce any large-scale public building projects in Paris. It seems, therefore, that the library has, after twenty years, set the seal on the 'Grands Projets de l'Etat'.

Let us first look back at the less recent past. Under Charles de Gaulle the town planning authorities' principal tasks during the 1950s and 1960s were the Villes Nouvelles of a 'Grande Couronne' on the periphery – satellite towns consisting of ribbon developments and high-rise blocks coupled with big arterial roads. The aim was to combat, in good time, a predicted housing shortage of dramatic proportions occasioned by a substantial influx into the capital and its environs. There came into being, up to twenty kilometres from the city centre, the new towns of Evry, Melun-Sénart, St.-Quentin-en-Yvelines, Cergy Pontoise, and Marne-la-Vallée, the home of Eurodisney. Each town was originally intended to house 500,000 inhabitants.

These new suburbs have produced no noteworthy innovations in the way of town planning. Although industrial concerns and service industries have moved in, many districts continue to retain the character of mass-populated dormitory towns. The desolate appearance of many 'Grands Ensembles', which lend themselves to unlimited expansion, has meant that many housing developments of this period are now occupied in isolation by the poorest sectors of the population, mostly immigrant families from North Africa.

During the 1970s it was the new Centre Beaubourg in the heart of Paris that caused a sensation unequalled since the building of the Eiffel Tower. In the Marais, parts of which had already undergone luxury redevelopment, the Italian Renzo Piano and the Briton Richard Rogers erected a brightly coloured, largely transparent 'culture machine' in steel. To the present-day observer its architecture seems the committed expression of an avowedly progressive period characterized by conformity with the requirements of a 'modern world' that would differ entirely from all that had gone before. To that extent, the Centre Beaubourg was a small-scale continuation of the megastructural urban visions of the 1960s. Its designers put their faith in experimentation, the utmost functional flexibility, and extremely complicated technical equipment. These basic ideas were proclaimed a structural credo by many other contemporary architects. The desire for novelty had also to be manifested – only symbolically, as a rule – in over-instrumented façades.

An object of fierce controversy, Piano's and Rogers's project threatened to founder. Today, its 'forward-looking' architectural language already seems antiquated. Nevertheless, this widely accessible building is one of the city's favourite venues for art exhibitions, houses a very popular though usually overcrowded municipal reference library, and constitutes a tourist attraction frequented by far more visitors than the planners had ever hoped. The forecourt has become a place of entertainment that now – dare I say it? –

seems as staple a feature of the French capital as the Place des Vosges or the open space above the Jardins du Trocadéro.

Every one of the 'Grands Projets' drew criticism from formidable opponents, though such strictures related generally to their expense and, in some cases, to the monumentality of their architecture. Twenty years after the Centre Beaubourg was built, Paris was thrown into a positive turmoil by the announcement of Mitterrand's last and, to him, most important 'Grand Projet'. Billions of francs were to be spent on his Bibliothèque Nationale de France. A gigantic 'book temple' near the Gare d'Austerlitz in the south-east of the city, it was to consist of four glass towers enclosing an open space and a huge, sunken inner courtyard designed to light the reading-rooms. This highly symbolic, almost book-sanctifying project had been rejected by its opponents not only because of the enormous expense involved but also on grounds of design and functional arrangement. In particular, many people were utterly mystified by the idea of locating a large proportion of the books in the glass towers' upper eleven storeys. The continuous filling of these store-rooms – a fascinating notion in the early design phase – will be impossible to observe from without because the books are kept in closed, air-conditioned containers obscured by folding wooden partitions. This fundamental conflict in the library's design will remain a bone of contention. Others criticize its site as well. They argue that the Seine is invisible from the raised, central square, and that this new public space, in which the architect made self-assured allusions to the Place du Palais-Royal, merely encompasses a big rectangular hole with treetops protruding from it.

Many users of scholarly libraries are already mourning the old Parisian reading-rooms, above all the unique Bibliothèque Nationale in the Rue de Richelieu, built in 1868 by Henri Labrouste. From 1997 onwards, all that will be perused beneath those lofty domes with their elegant iron columns are manuscripts, prints, and rarities. The fate of other small libraries in Paris is uncertain. Sceptics predict further amalgamations when the new library opens with an immense expenditure on running costs.

Mitterrand did not react to criticism of the library and his other building projects. He remained unmoved by it, at least outwardly, but lost no opportunity to proclaim, with rhetorical skill, that the 'Grands Projets' symbolized his commitment to the nation and the preservation of France's cultural heritage. His projects would, he said, help to create central locations in the city where people could obtain knowledge of the roots and history of their country and the world at large. This was not the expression of a striving for intellectual prestige, but a genuine desire on the part of a president who recognized and skilfully exploited the new importance

Dominique Perrault, Bibliothèque Nationale François Mitterrand, 1992–96, detail

attaching to culture in France 'so that the nation can identify itself once more'. And he added: 'In order to emerge from the crisis, a cultural infrastructure is of great importance.'

But the 'Grand Projets' also disclose something different and altogether crucial: Mitterrand's hankering after immortality. 'Yes, I like history, and I like leaving traces in history. People remember Tutankhamun. What will they say in a few thousand years even of Charles de Gaulle, Georges Pompidou, Valérie Giscard d'Estaing, of me?' (Mitterrand in April 1995). Architecture mattered to him because of its inherent symbolism. Buildings are enduring monuments to greatness and perfection. Mitterrand was reputed to take a downright combative view of ephemerality, hence his unequalled desire to leave behind a token of his great days as President of France. That his last trip abroad, made not long before he died, should have taken him to Egypt, a country he had visited many times before, exemplifies his passion for the great civilizations of the past. To quote François Chaslin, former editor of *L'Architecture d'Aujourd'hui* in Paris: '...this remarkable head of state who liked to be compared to a sphinx, this King of the Left, a republican monarch' succeeded in 'evolving a socialist variant of the sovereign with a surprising, individual character'. The satirical press coined the appellation 'Mitteramses I'. Although it may be too daring to relate the basic geometrical conformation of Ieoh

Ming Pei's glass pyramid at the Louvre to Mitterrand's beloved Egypt, he must undoubtedly have been impressed by the adoption of such an emphatic, timeless shape for the new entrance to the museum, one of France's 'national shrines'.

Mitterrand announced his Louvre project at the very first press conference he held after his election in May 1981. Many failed to recognize the long-time leader of the French Left in his new capacity: once elected to the presidency, he set some surprising targets. The Grande Louvre and the new national library were 'his' most important cultural projects. Criticism of the relatively small glass pyramid in the Cour Napoléon, which was not confined to France, has since subsided. Today, though considerably enlarged by the Richelieu Wing, the world's biggest museum can scarcely cope with the swarms of visitors it attracts.

Mitterrand's keen interest in architecture was evident from his personal visits to building sites. He often looked in at the site of 'his' library in company with Dominique Perrault, the architect whose winning design he had selected, to check on current progress. These meetings were important to Perrault. Mitterrand asked specific questions and made occasional suggestions. What interested him most of all was whether the architect had faith in what he was doing. Perrault recalled in an interview that the President once asked him, rather anxiously: 'Are you sure that what you're doing will be good? If you think it's good, make a good job of it.'

The intensity of Mitterrand's desire to bequeathe posterity something 'imperishable' through the medium of these buildings is also apparent from quite another project which he not only initiated but inaugurated shortly before the end of his presidency: the European Archaeological Centre at Glux-en-Glenne in Burgundy. This institution, which embodies a research centre and a small museum, was designed by the Parisian architect Pierre-Louis Faloci and described by Mitterrand as a 'Grand Projet de l'Etat en Province'. Situated at the foot of Mont Beuvray was the Celtic city of Bibracte, a sporadically excavated archaeological site from which no more startling discoveries can be expected. References to Bibracte in history books relate largely to battles, and De bello gallico implies that Caesar defeated the Helvetii near there in 58 B.C. Six years later the Celtic prince Vercingetorix mustered the Gallic tribes at Bibracte in an attempt to resist Roman supremacy – an undertaking in which he failed despite the assistance of the crafty comic-book hero Asterix and his bosom pal Obelix.

In 1985 Mitterrand declared the whole of Mont Beuvray, which was situated in his old Burgundian constituency (he was also mayor of Château-Chinon), a 'Site National' or protected area. As in Paris, so in the provinces, he planned to insure his posthumous reputation by means of cultural investments. He also considered selecting the summit of Mont Beuvray, the 800-metre-high site of the Celtic hero's victory, as his burial-place. (He was, in fact, buried at Jarnac, his place of birth near Cognac, and no one knows if his wish for a lofty tomb and monument atop the Celts' mountain will ever be fulfilled.)

Because of their inherent symbolism, Mitterrand's public works occupy a special place in the Parisian scene. The decision to carry out these large-scale projects rested solely with the president, who speeded their planning and ensured that they were fully funded in almost every case. No parliamentary approval was needed, and the city itself had little opportunity to meddle in the plans of whichever president was in office. Central government had always made heavy inroads into the fabric of the French capital, with the result that municipal building policy was that of the state, never of the city itself. It was not until 1977 that Paris acquired a mayor invested with real authority: Jacques Chirac, leader of the Gaullist Party and, from the end of 1995, Mitterrand's successor in office. Chirac was the first to dispute with a president over building projects. Valéry Giscard d'Estaing, who meddled in plans for the former site of Les Halles and wanted something different, was overruled. Giscard's 'history-conscious' ideas on architecture were allied with theatrical exaggerations on the part of Ricardo Bofill, who was to develop the quarter, and the President failed to get his way. Town planning suddenly became a bone of contention, because Giscard and Mayor Chirac were at that time two major rivals on the French political Right. The 'Grands Projets' were originally intended to form part of a world exhibition to mark the 200th anniversary of the French Revolution, but this idea was abandoned in 1983.

Although the capital has now been legally an independent urban community for nearly twenty years, it continues to be controlled by the state. Mitterrand accepted this situation by seeking the city fathers' approval of his schemes at the very beginning of his presidency. The only 'Grand Projet' to be blocked was an International Conference Centre on the Quai Branly, near the foot of the Eiffel Tower. The three glass cubes were designed in detail by the Parisian architect Francis Soler but rejected after protests from residents in that middle-class and, thus, influential part of the city. Moreover, the need for such a conference centre was disputed from the outset.

In 1986, five years after Mitterrand's election to the presidency, there began the period of 'cohabitation' during which, for the first time in the history of the Fifth Republic, a left-wing president and a right-wing premier were obliged to co-operate. This had an influence on the 'Grands Projets'. The government disliked promoting buildings whose sole purpose, as they saw it, was to advertise Mitterrand's prestige. However, the work was already completed or so far advanced that no scheme was abandoned, though delays occurred in the case of the Parc de la Villette.

It must in retrospect be stated that some of the buildings in the 'Grands Projets' programme, for instance the Institut du Monde Arabe, did not score as great a success as, say, the Grande Louvre. Jean Nouvel's architecture is fascinating, but the low ceilings in the office areas do not favour good working conditions, the 27,000 photoelectric blinds in the façades are extremely malfunction-prone, and the roof terrace restaurant has had to be closed for want of customers.

The Gare d'Orsay, which was converted under Giscard d'Estaing into a museum for 19th-century art, continues to attract strong criticism. The original intention was to demolish the disused station to make way for a hotel. Once the decision had been taken to convert it, Gae Aulenti's plan was put into effect. Very self-assertively, if not downright overweeningly, she transformed the central bay into a thoroughfare. She failed, however, to master the problem of scale, and her small, built-in exhibition rooms are reminiscent of the entrances to Egyptian burial chambers. The Ministry of Finance, a long, clumsy slab situated at an angle to the Seine, is urbanistically dubious, and its monumental façades make a forbidding impression. It is an exception in other respects as well. Not a public building in the cultural sense, it was needed because of the ministry's removal from the Richelieu Wing of the Louvre. Controversy continued to surround it long after its completion. Chirac and Balladur, the then minister of finance, did not want the new ministry and delayed the move considerably.

Despite initial incomprehension and, in some cases, vigorous protests on the part of large sections of the population, nearly all the 'Grands Projets' have at least found acceptance. They are the goal of visitors from all over France and abroad. To tourists, these projects now constitute attractions like the Eiffel Tower or Montmartre. Even the Opéra de la Bastille, disastrously though its dimensions impinge on a square steeped in history and architecturally mediocre though it is, both outside and in, draws good houses despite the high prices charged by what was heralded as a 'people's opera'. As for the Grande Arche in the business quarter of La Défense, it has become a popular destination for family outings on Sundays.

Modern Paris is the only city in Europe of which it can justly be said that, even today, an intact and unique urban landscape has been successfully amplified and enhanced by means of large-scale buildings. It may indeed be the city's very wealth of urban qualities from the past that has enabled it to be augmented with large-scale projects of this kind.

Francis Soler, International Conference Centre, Quai Branly, project 1992

Lageplan der Projekte

Errata

Due to an error at the printer's, the titles listed in the key on page 26 were left in the German original. Please find below the English translation for the **Location of the Projects**.

Location of the Projects

ST-DENIS
VILLENEUVE-LA-GARENNE
Aéroport Charles de Gaulle 12 km
Av. du Gén. de Gaulle
Av. de Verdun
Cathédrale St-Denis
LE BOURGET
GENNEVILLIERS
Av. de la Div. Leclerc
LA COURNEUVE
Bd Pasteur
Av. Marceau
DRANCY
21
Quai de Seine
Av. P. V. Couturier
ST-OUEN
R. de Stalingrad
R. du Landy
Quai Aulagnier
Av. Henri Barbusse
AUBERVILLIERS
Quai de Clichy
V. Hugo
Av. Jean Jaurès
BOBIGNY
Bd Jean Jaurès
CLICHY
Bd
Porte de la Chapelle
Av. V. Hugo
Av. de la République
Gén. Leclerc
Rue V. Hugo
Av. du
R. de Paris
MONTMARTRE
19
18
Bd Périphérique
PANTIN
R. du Parc
Av. de St-Ouen
20
Av. J. Lolive
Av. de Clichy
Cim. de Montmartre
Parc de la Villette / Cité des Sciences et de l'Industrie
ROMAINVILLE
Porte d'Asnières
Sacré-Cœur
R. de Flandre
17
Av. J. Jaurès
Bd Malesherbes
Gare du Nord
16
R. de Paris
Gare St-Lazare
Buttes-Chaumont
Porte des Lilas
Arc de Triomphe
Bd
Haussmann
Gare de l'Est
Rue de Belleville
Av. des Champs-Elysées
Opéra-Garnier
BELLEVILLE
Bd Mortier
Av. Kléber
Pl. de la République
15
Belleville
BAGNOLET
Bd de Sébastopol
14
Porte de Bagnolet
Av. de New York
Av. de la République
13
Quai d'Orsay
Rue de Rivoli
Quai des Tuileries
Centre Pompidou
MONTREUIL
1
Louvre
Bd Davout
Tour Eiffel
Cimetière du Père-Lachaise
Bd Voltaire
Av. de Suffren
Hôtel des Invalides
Bd
Saint-
Notre-Dame
R. de Paris
Pl. de la Bastille
Rue du Fg. St-Antoine
VINCENNES
Bd
Germain
Opéra-Bastille
Pl. de la Nation
Cours de Vincennes
Porte de Vincennes
Raspail
Quai St Bernard
Gare de Lyon
Av. de Paris
Bd du Montparnasse
Château de Vincennes
Gare Austerlitz
Av. Daumesnil
Rue Lecourbe
Rue de Vaugirard
Gare Montparnasse
3
4
Parc Floral
Av. du Maine
5
6
Convention
10
Bd de l'Hôpital
7
Quai de la Gare
Porte de Versailles
8
Bois de Vincennes
Porte d'Italie
Bd Lefebvre
Av. du Gén. Leclerc
Lac Daumesnil
Bd Brune
Rue de Tolbiac
Quai d'Ivry
Porte d'Orléans
Av. d' Italie
Quai M. Boyer
CHARENTON
Vincennes
Av. P. Brossolette
9
Av. de Gravelle
MONTROUGE
Av. de Verdun
Noisy-le-Grand 10 km
Av. de Fontainebleau
Seine
Av. Aristide Briand
CHÂTILLON
Cim. Parisien de Bagneux
LE KREMLIN-BICÊTRE
MAISONS-ALFORT
Aéroport Orly 10 km

La Grande Arche

Johan Otto von Spreckelsen with Paul Andreu

Competition 1983
Constructed 1984–9

It was in the late 1950s, a period marked by great faith in the future, that plans were laid for 'La Défense', a commercial and residential centre to be developed north-west of Paris on the site of the then village suburbs of Puteaux and Courbevoie. Its name derives from the monument erected there to the 'défenseurs' of Paris who fought the Prussians in 1871.

Building work began in the 1960s. The central axis of approach was a precise extension of the 'royal axis' that begins in the Louvre's Cour Carrée and leads out of the city by way of the Champs-Elysées and the Avenue Charles de Gaulle. The aim was to construct a modern, uncluttered, ultra-efficient urban centre covering 750 hectares, so its various functions were separated accordingly. People can move about freely on a central plateau 100 metres wide and 1.4 kilometres long, the terraced 'parvis' that leads down to the Seine and the centre of Paris. This huge expanse of concrete is articulated with squares, green spaces, and eye-catching artistic installations by – among others – Alexander Calder, Piotr Kowalski, and Aiko Miyawaki, together with a fountain designed by Yaacov Agam. Cars skirt the high-rise town on six-lane urban motorways and disappear into huge underground garages. Although augmented year after year by more towers of bluish, greenish, or reflecting glass, La Défense continues to be perfectly accessible by road as well as by RER and suburban trains.

Paris's 'Little Manhattan', whose skyline is clearly visible from the Arc de Triomphe in clear conditions, has failed in its attempt to define urban space by architectural means. Although it is far enough from the inner city for buildings to be freely disposed, this freedom is fraught with constraints. Seen from the 'national royal axis', the vista of commonplace, high-rise office blocks at first aroused protests, but people have since grown accustomed to the skyline. La Défense has become a living centre. The 'parvis' presents an animated picture even on Sundays – and not only when a children's sports day has been arranged or when some motor manufacturer is using the expanse as as effective backdrop for the presentation of a new model.

Soon after planning began it became clear that La Défense needed an emblem of some kind – a symbolic building that would form the extremity of the axis and enable the district to identify with it. The result was the Grande Arche, or Great Arch, that so strikingly terminates the whole complex. A duplication of the Arc de Triomphe translated into the present day, this 'Tête de la Défense' may almost be said to symbolize the city on equal terms. Not a celebration of military successes like the triumphal arches of antiquity, it stands for the triumph of the office society. The building was finished in time for the 200th anniversary of the French Revolution.

The international competition, which attracted 424 entries, was won in 1983 by the Danish architect Johan Otto von Spreckelsen. His huge open cube occupies the end of the big 'parvis'. The big visual axis ends abruptly just beyond the building, but it is planned to extend it for another five kilometres to the site of yet another commercial centre. What form and dimensions will the new terminative building assume? Something gigantic is to be expected.

Closer inspection of Spreckelsen's building reveals that its overwhelming bulk is really composed of two 35-storey office blocks only 19 metres wide. With a height of 110 metres and an overall width of 106, however, the building is made by means of its chamfered 'roof' to resemble a hollow cube. By adopting a hollow rather than a solid conformation, Spreckelsen cleverly obviated the danger of terminating the royal axis altogether and left scope for future extensions. The building had to be offset by 6°30 because the foundations could not otherwise have been accommodated between the railway lines and roads below ground. This enables the distant observer to perceive something of the depth of the block. A flight of steps leads between the sides of the building, both of which are chamfered at an angle of 45°, from the 'parvis' to the block's 'inner square', which is overlooked by the office façades on the inner sides of the cube. In the midst of this open expanse – except when service is suspended because of bad weather – four glass lifts glide silently up and down. Visitors can only reach the building's 'belvédère', or panoramic viewing platform, by means of these circular glass cabins, which disappear into the underside of the roof. In the roof space itself, separated by four open courtyards, are exhibition spaces and presentation rooms. The floors of the courtyards, each measuring 400 square metres, are decorated with a celestial map by Jean-Pierre Raynaud. Fragmentary signs of the zodiac in black granite are inlaid in expanses of white marble slabs.

The 'clouds' suspended above the open cube's inner courtyard and held taut by steel cables were originally planned in glass but executed in sheets of white plastic on grounds of expense. Designed by the engineer Paul Andreu,

View along the central axis of the office, business and residential district of La Défense, with the Grande Arche in the background.

the sail is there, like the sheets of glass erected in the open space inside the block, to break the wind that comes rushing through the huge aperture. Situated beneath the 'clouds' is the central entrance that leads to the RER station and the exhibition rooms housed in the base.

The load-bearing structure consists of a big arch of pre-stressed ferroconcrete: four building-high frames occupying the full depth of each slab like ladders whose rungs support the floor decks. Stabilization against wind pressure is provided by the connecting roof. The inner surfaces of the open cube are smooth and faced with white Carrara marble; the window surfaces, by contrast, are heavily structured. The square openings are inset in niches and vertically divided into zones of seven storeys. The ladder supports are visible as continuous vertical bands.

The architect suffered a disappointment while work was in progress. Powerless to intervene, he was compelled to see the monument he had designed as 'humanity's triumphal arch' down-graded for political reasons into an unadorned, purely functional building. He thereupon withdrew from the project and entrusted its further supervision to Paul Andreu. The upper levels and the base do, for all that, offer plenty of room for exhibitions.

In 1989 Jean Nouvel designed a tower 400 metres high for a small site north-west of the Grande Arche. This circular glass structure, which would greatly have detracted from the Grande Arche's present dominance, is not to be built.
S.R.

The Grande Arche comprises two 19 metre high office tower blocks, linked by a multistorey roof element. Access for visitors to the exhibition rooms and the panoramic viewing platform is via the separate lift tower.

New office towers are being built every year along the length of the 'parvis'. The installation (centre) is by the Japanese sculptor Aiko Miyawaki.

Le Grand Louvre

Ieoh Ming Pei, Michel Macary, Italo Rota, Gérard Grandval, Jean-Michel Wilmotte

Constructed 1985–6

The Louvre consists of two buildings dating from different periods. It was under Louis XIII that there originated the idea of demolishing the castle on the left bank of the Seine, where Philip II, surnamed Augustus, had erected a 12th-century predecessor: a square fortification incorporated in the city wall and, during the 14th century, developed into a citadel by Charles V. A much larger square was marked out but not developed until the reign of Louis XIV by the architect and noted 'metteur-en-scène' Louis Le Vau, and, later, by Claude Perrault. The massive colonnades on the east side of the complex, which Perrault erected after an unscrupulous contest with Gianlorenzo Bernini, were designed to demonstrate the superiority of French classicism over Roman baroque. Two storeys high, this immense row of columns indicates that the king meant to use the Louvre primarily for ceremonial purposes, not as a royal residence. Although larger in terms of volume than everything constructed before, the additions made under Napoleon I, during the Second Republic, under Napoleon III, and, lastly, during the Third Republic, were merely westward extensions of the complex along the axis of symmetry. Today, the two wings designed by the architects Visconti and Lefuel project as far as the Avenue du Général Lemonnier.

The National Convention opened the Louvre as a central art museum for the French nation in 1793. The Cour Napoléon project aroused fierce controversy during the 1980s, and not among the inhabitants of Paris alone.

Nobody disputed that the Louvre, one of the world's largest and most important museums, was no longer equal to its task. The ever-growing collections could not be satisfactorily displayed or stored, nor was it possible to channel the streams of visitors. The 'miracle solution' directly commissioned from Ieoh Ming Pei, New York's star architect of Chinese extraction, consisted in excavating a large area of the centrally located Cour Napoléon and capping it in the middle with a pyramid 22 metres high and 35 metres square at the base. Visible from afar, this marks the main entrance. Visitors are not distributed among various entrances but directed into the big subterranean reception hall and from there into the wings. Pei's emphatic glass structure successfully defines this new entrance. Ideally situated in the central courtyard, it provides access to all the Louvre's wings and the exposed remains of the ancient fortifications.

The rearrangement of accesses was a matter of special concern once it became established, after much argument, that the staff of the Ministry of Finance were to move out of the Louvre's north wing and into a new building in the Bercy district of Paris.

Despite its spectacular location, the pyramid itself is small compared to the buildings around it. The criticism that it would compete with the old Louvre's façades and obscure them too greatly has not been borne out. Far more substantial than this glass icon in the courtyard is the area beneath it, the subterranean entrance hall whose dimensions cannot be surmised from above. Its architectural conformation and well-devised access plan, together with the consummate workmanship of its floors, walls, and steps in big slabs of pale stone, bear witness to the quality of its design and lend it a lavish appearance. Measuring 200 × 120 metres, it is the new Louvre's most monumental enclosed space and houses the central information desk, turnstiles leading to clearly marked entrances, shops selling books and souvenirs, a post office, several restaurants, and an auditorium. The pyramid and hall were opened in time for the bicentenary of the French Revolution in 1989.

'Le Carrousel du Louvre', an underground passage leading in the direction of the Jardin des Tuileries, was added not long ago. Terminating in a spacious bus station and car park, also underground, this is flanked by luxury shops selling objets d'art and punctuated at the half-way mark by an inverted glass pyramid – a companion piece to the pyramid above the main entrance.

The Richelieu Wing, occupied until 1989 by the Ministry of Finance, runs parallel to Rue de Rivoli for 195 metres. The rooms behind its neo-Renaissance façade were only 3.5 metres high, which meant that the two lower ranges of windows were divided by intermediate floors. Chief planner Ieoh Ming Pei and the architects Michel Macary and Jean-Michel Wilmotte, who had been entrusted with the conversion, managed to gut the building without altering its exterior. Except in a few places, all the floors were torn out to create two storeys 7 metres high out of four low-ceilinged ones. A further complete museum storey was gained by heightening the attics. To the right and left of the massive central section, vaulted glass roofs designed by Peter Rice were erected over the three inner courtyards. These courtyards, the Cour Marly, the Cour Puget, and the smaller Cour

Ein neues Wahrzeichen von Paris, das heute wie selbstverständlich dazugehört: die Pyramide des New Yorker Architekten Ieoh Ming Pei.

telrisalits wurden die drei Innenhöfe nach Entwürfen von Peter Rice mit gewölbten Glasdächern überbaut. Diese Höfe, die Cour Marly, die Cour Puget und die kleinere Cour Khorsabad, stellen die imposantesten Räume des neuen Museumsflügels dar. Ausgestellt sind hier französische Skulpturen aus dem 17. und 18. Jahrhundert. Die berühmten frühklassizistischen Pferde von Marly von Guillaume Coustou, die früher an der Place de la Concorde standen, flankieren nun eine ausladende Treppe, die zu einer umlaufenden Galerie führt. Auch die anderen zum Teil sehr großen Skulpturen wurden zwanglos gruppiert und kommen durch den großzügig bemessenen Luftraum gut zur Geltung. Die Absenkung der Hofflächen ermöglichte eine unterirdische Verbindung zwischen den Höfen. Der Raumeindruck ist dadurch noch monumentaler. In der Cour Khorsabad stehen 30 Tonnen schwere geflügelte Stiere sowie Reliefs und Fragmente der Palastfassaden des Assyrer-Königs Sargon II. aus dem 8. Jahrhundert v. Chr.. 165 Ausstellungsräume mit rund 1200 Skulpturen, Kleinplastiken, Gobelins etc. vom späten 18. und 19. Jahrhundert sowie Kunstschätze des Altertums und der Malerei von der Gotik bis Nicolas Poussin gruppieren sich um die Höfe und füllen das Attikageschoß. Das Untergeschoß wurde von den Architekten wie ein Gewölbekeller gestaltet. Dort fand sich Platz für die lichtempfindlichen Textilien und Buchmalereien der islamischen Kunst. Im ersten Obergeschoß blieb die opulent im Historismus gestaltete Suite von Napoleon III. erhalten. Sie hatte zuvor als Empfangsraum für das Finanzministerium gedient. Die Büroräume des Ministers wurden zu einem Museumscafé umgestaltet.

Die bewegte Geschichte des im Herzen der Stadt liegenden Grand Louvre hat mit spektakulären Ergänzungen und Eingriffen der Architekten eine ›Vitalisierung‹ erfahren, und die Ausstellungsflächen wurden verdoppelt. 200 Jahre nach seiner Gründung wird zum ersten Mal die gesamte geschlossene U-Form der Schloßanlage als Museum genutzt. Jetzt bleibt die Frage, ob es gelingt, bei weiter steigenden Besucherzahlen in der riesigen Kulturmaschine noch einen stillen Platz für den stillen Genuß der Kunstschätze zu finden.

S.R.

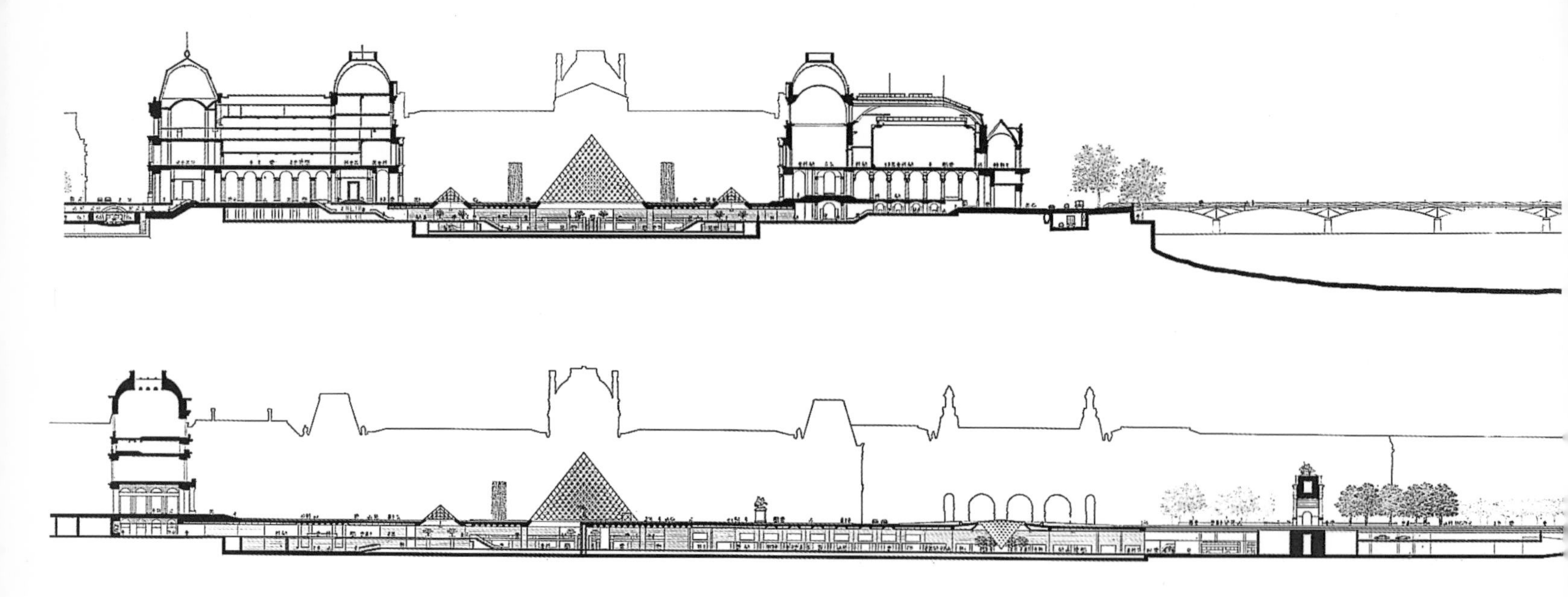

Quer- und Längsschnitt durch den Grand Louvre mit der Pyramide.

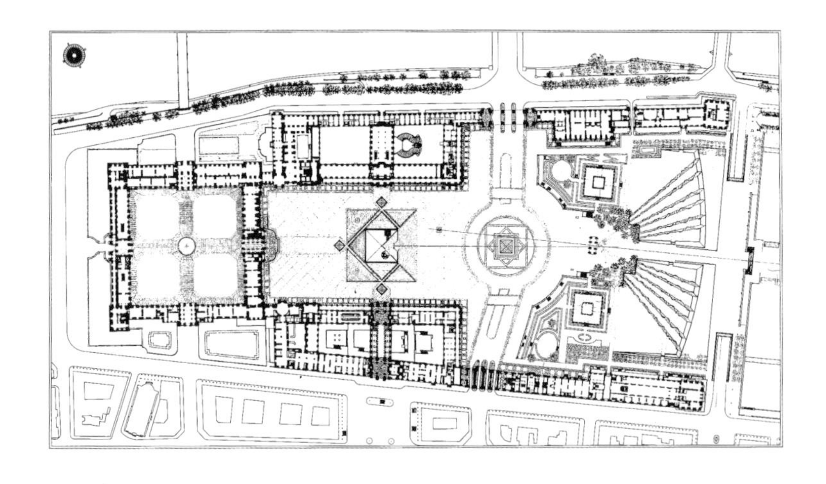

Grundrisse von Ober- und Untergeschoß des gesamten Grand Louvre. Das Untergeschoß verdeutlicht die Größe der unterirdischen Erschließungsbereiche mit Hörsaal, Läden, Restaurants und Parkplätzen.

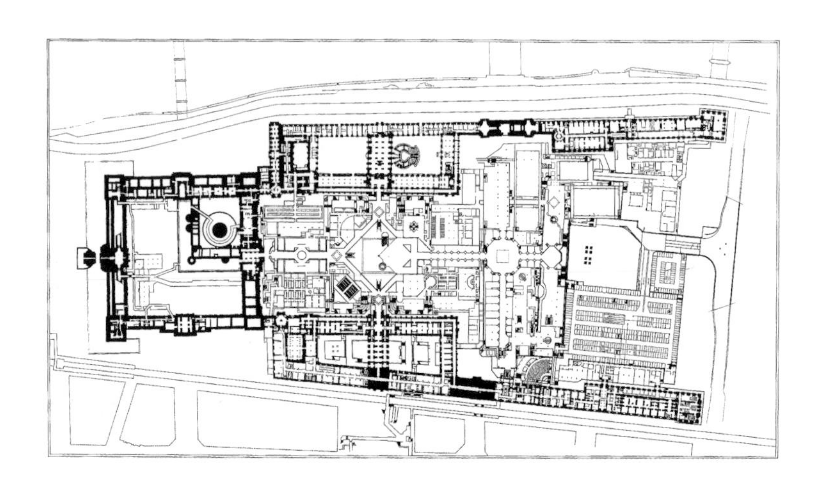

Die Pyramide ist umgeben von Wasserbassins, die von Wegen durchschnitten werden. Der Glaskörper hat eine Höhe von knapp 22 Metern und eine Seitenlänge von 35 Metern. Er wiegt 80 Tonnen.

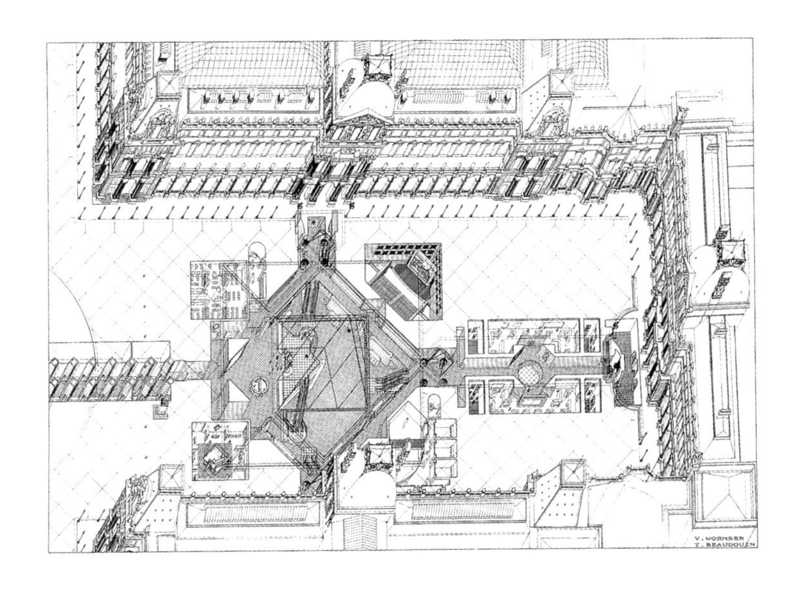
V. WORMSER
T. BEAUDOUIN

Die Halle ist umgeben von einem Hörsaal, Restaurants und einer Buchhandlung. Eine Ladenpassage endet an einer kleinen, auf dem Kopf stehenden Pyramide.

Die unterirdische zentrale Erschließungshalle des Grand Louvre. Die Besucher teilen sich hier auf und gelangen in die drei Flügelbauten Sully, Denon und Richelieu sowie zu den alten Befestigungsanlagen unter dem Cour Carrée aus der Zeit von König Philippe II. Auguste (um 1200 n.Chr.)

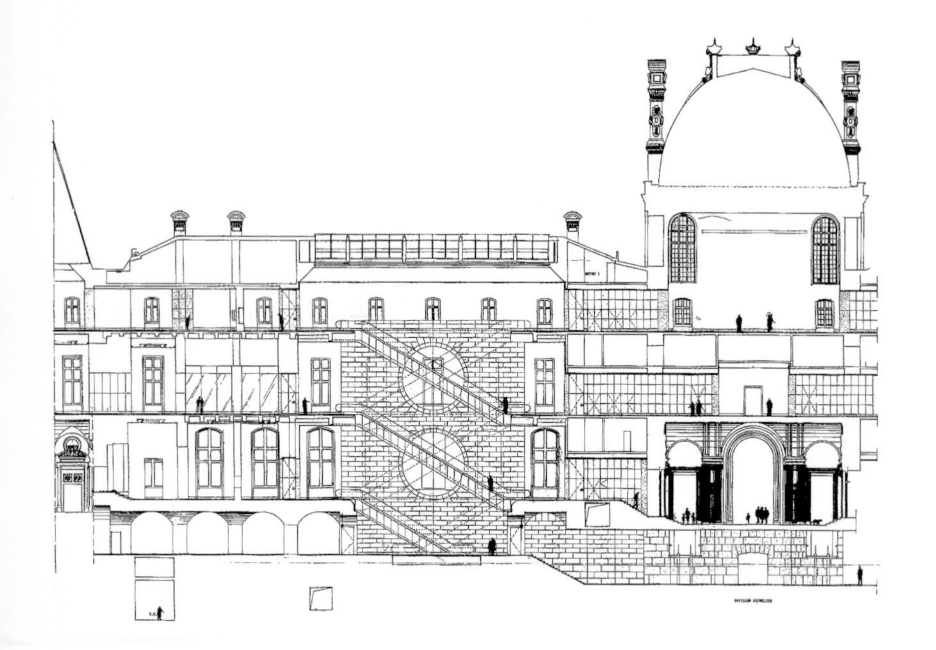

Im Richelieu-Flügel befand sich zuvor das Finanzministerium. Nach dessen Auszug wurden die beiden großen Innenhöfe mit Glasdächern versehen. Der auf diese Weise gewonnene Raum wird jetzt für die Skulpturensammlung des Klassizismus genutzt.

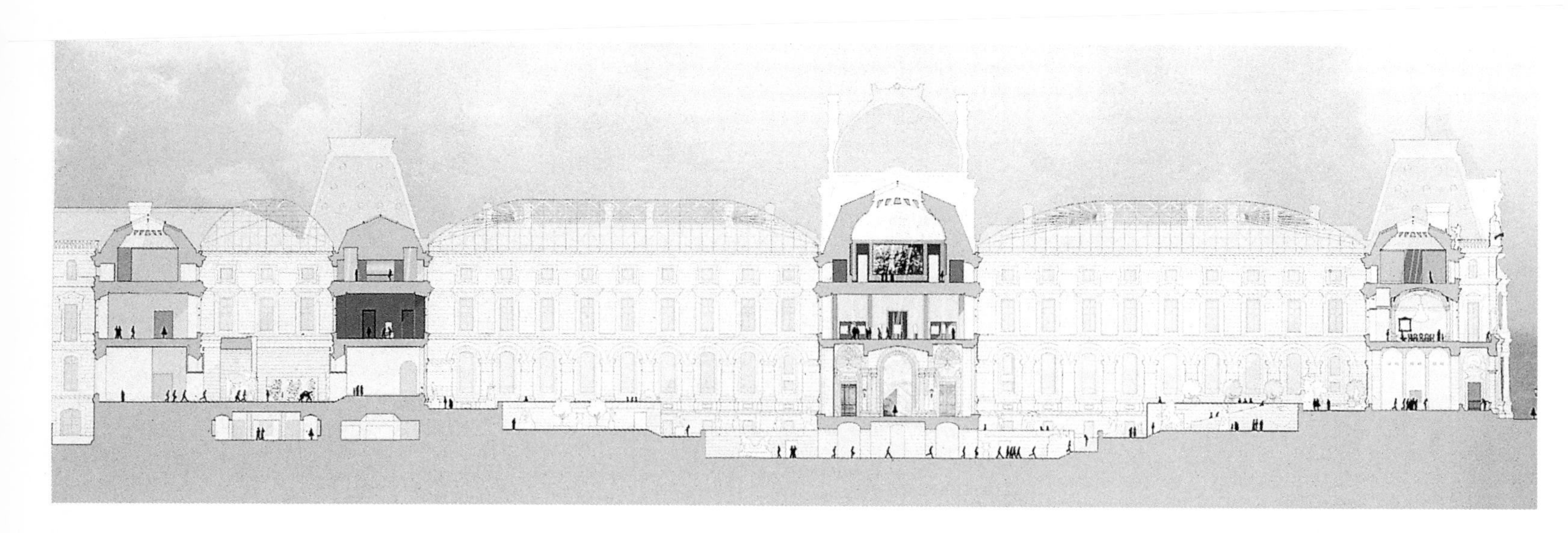

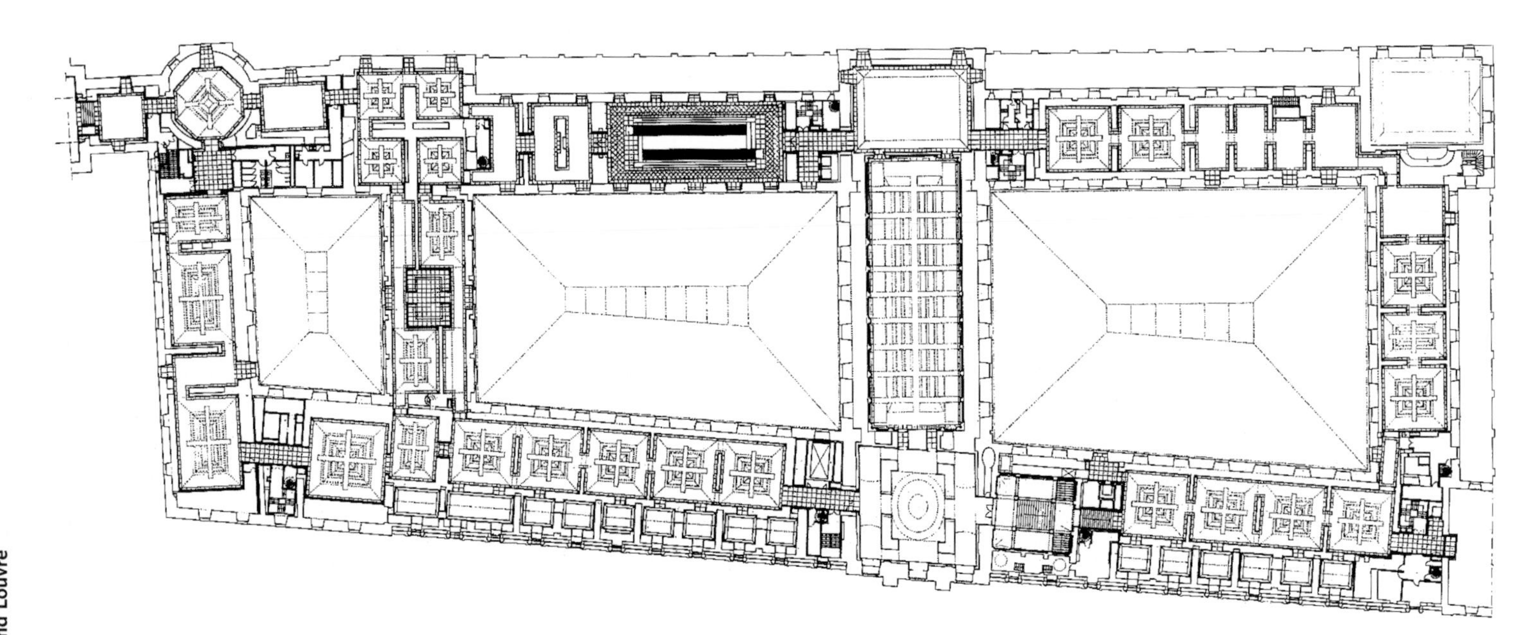

Einblicke in die teilweise völlig neu in den Richelieu-Flügel eingefügten Ausstellungsräume des Museums.

Bibliothèque Nationale François Mitterrand

Dominique Perrault

Wettbewerb 1989
Bauzeit 1992–96

Paris verfügt über wunderbare alte Bibliotheksgebäude, deren Lesesäle noch im Originalzustand erhalten sind. Besonders hervorzuheben sind die Bibliothèque Nationale in der Rue de Richelieu und die Bibliothèque Sainte Geneviève am Pantheon, die im 19. Jahrhundert von Henri Labrouste erbaut wurden. Sie sind jedoch zu klein geworden und entsprechen nicht mehr den heutigen Anforderungen von Nutzern wissenschaftlicher Bibliotheken.

Nach 14jähriger Amtszeit sorgte Frankreichs Staatspräsident François Mitterrand für ein Abschiedsgeschenk der Superlative, das diese Mängel beheben sollte: die neue Bibliothèque Nationale, in der bis zu 12 Millionen Bücher Platz finden. Mitterrand war es auch vergönnt, am 30. März 1995, nur wenige Wochen vor seinem Auszug aus dem Elyséepalast, die noch leeren Hallen feierlich einzuweihen. Die offizielle Eröffnung fand Ende 1996 statt. Die neue Bibliothèque Nationale dient als zentrale Forschungsbibliothek Frankreichs und als allgemeine Informationsbibliothek, bei der der Zugang zu den Beständen ungehindert möglich ist: ein im Ansatz problematisches Konzept, da ein Massenbetrieb möglicherweise nicht ausbleiben wird

1989 fand ein Wettbewerb für den Neubau statt, an dem zwanzig Architekten teilnahmen, die zuvor von einem Gremium ausgewählt worden waren. Dominique Perrault aus Paris, damals gerade 36 Jahre alt, gewann überraschend mit einem äußerst klaren und prägnanten Konzept. Vier winkelförmige Ecktürme stehen sich wie vier geöffnete Bücher gegenüber und begrenzen einen symbolischen Raum. Die Hochhäuser, die zunächst 100 Meter hoch werden sollten und dann auf 79 Meter reduziert wurden, sollen die Ansammlung von Wissen oder auch die Ansammlung unerreichter Kenntnis repräsentieren. In den Erläuterungen des Architekten finden sich bildhafte Bezeichnungen wie Büchertürme, Silo, Riesen-Bücherregale oder vertikale Labyrinthe. Die Türme gliedern sich in verschiedene Zonen. Sechs Bürogeschosse, dann zehn Magazin- und zwei Technikgeschosse. Nur knapp die Hälfte des gesamten Buchmagazins auf einer Regallänge von 400 km befindet sich – entgegen der ursprünglichen Planung – in den Türmen; der Rest ist im Sockel hinter den Lesesälen gelagert. Gefüllt oder leer – in den Türmen sind die Bücher von außen nicht wahrzunehmen, da hinter der doppelten Verglasung und den aufklappbaren Holzelementen aus Gründen des Licht- und Feuerschutzes eine weitere Wand eingebaut wurde. Die Entwurfsidee des Architekten, daß von außen erlebt werden kann, wie sich über Jahre hinweg das Magazin in den Glastürmen füllt, mußte damit verworfen werden.

Die Bücher transportiert das automatisierte System ›Télédoc‹. Das bestellte Dokument wird in eine Box gelegt, die von einem kleinen Schienenwagen zur Ausgabestelle gefahren wird. Die vertikalen Schienenstränge der Türme führen in die Technikzone, die die Sockelgeschosse wie ein Gürtel umschließt. Von dort zweigen die Schienen in die Lesesäle ab. Vom obersten Magazingeschoß eines Turmes bis zur am weitesten entfernten Ausgabestelle dauert die Fahrt zwölf Minuten (durchschnittliche Fahrtdauer nur viereinhalb Minuten). Wer schon weiß, wann er welche Titel wo lesen will, reserviert Bücher und Leseplatz bereits an seinem heimischen ›Minitel‹ und kommt zum festgelegten Termin in die Bibliothek.

Die Gesamtwirkung des Neubaus bestimmen weniger die Baukörper als der durch die vier Ecktürme definierte leere Raum. Zwischen den Türmen ist wie ein Plateau der zentrale Platz eingehängt, der in seiner Größe der Place de la Concorde entspricht. In der Mitte liegt tief unten der zentrale Hof der Bibliothek, den der Architekt »einen Klostergarten der Ruhe und Besinnlichkeit« nennt. Es gelang hier zum ersten Mal, ausgewachsene Nadelbäume aus einer Waldschonung zu verpflanzen. Die 120 Kiefern sind bis zu vierzig Jahre alt, haben eine Höhe von zwanzig Metern und wiegen pro Baum ca. zwölf Tonnen. Die Bäume wurden bereits drei Jahre vorher in einem Wald in der Normandie ausgewählt und auf den Transport vorbereitet. Nach der Umpflanzung werden sie noch für lange Zeit mit Stahlseilen gehalten.

Der Besucher der Bibliothek betritt zunächst die gigantische Freitreppe des Sockels. An den Schmalseiten des Terrains folgen Aluminiumrahmen. Der Platz – Esplanade genannt – wie auch die Treppenanlage wurden mit wetterfesten Bohlen aus Tropenholz versehen, was bei Naturschützern für heftige Proteste sorgte. Über Rampen an den kurzen Seiten des zentralen Hofs gelangt der Besucher dann zu den tieferliegenden zwei Haupteingängen. Trotz des regen Besucherverkehrs wird der weiträumige und zugige Platz kein Ort zum Verweilen werden. Er symbolisiert eher im Sinne von Mitterrand die Größe von »Frankreichs Wissen«, das hier aufbewahrt wird. Der Ausblick ist nur zur Seine hin mit dem gegenüberliegenden Parc de Bercy reizvoll. Ansonsten ist der Platz, den der Architekt als einen öffentlichen Erlebnisraum plante, nur ein Umgang entlang den Absperrungen zum Innenhof und bleibt für die verwöhnten Flaneure von Paris ohne Bedeutung. Die Lesesäle, Veranstaltungsräume und Restaurants sind auf zwei Ebenen um den Hof gruppiert. Die

Die vier gläsernen Büchertürme definieren eine neue Platzanlage oberhalb der Seine. In ihrer Mitte liegt tief unten der zentrale Hof der Bibliothek.

obere ist öffentlich zugänglich, die untere für Wissenschaftler und Forscher mit Voranmeldung bestimmt, die auch in Einzelkabinen arbeiten können. Je 18 voll verkabelte Zellen sind auf den quer den unteren Lesesaal überspannenden und in den Umgang hineinragenden Brücken zusammengefaßt. Die Benutzer können sich hier hinter verglasten ›Visierschlitzen‹ verschanzen. Bevor sie ihre Leseplätze erreicht haben, erwartet sie nach dem Durchschreiten der oberen Empfangssäle zunächst eine ›Schlucht‹, die in ihrer Dramatik in der Architekturgeschichte kaum ihresgleichen hat. Mehr als 30 Meter hoch, winkelförmig, die Wände mit großen dunklen Stahlmattengobelins behängt, gleitet der Leser via Rolltreppe nach unten in den Büchertempel. Das Stahlgewebe an den Wänden findet normalerweise in der Sieb- und Filtertechnik sowie in der Luft- und Raumfahrttechnik Verwendung. Wer von diesem Raumerlebnis zu überwältigt ist, um sich sogleich seinen Büchern widmen zu können, den erwarten im ›Club chercheur‹ bequeme Sessel in entspannter Atmosphäre.

Perrault verwendete das ungewöhnliche Stahlgewebe auch als Material für die abgehängten Decken. In den großen Lesesälen werden die Bahnen quergespannt und hängen aufgrund ihrer Elastizität durch. Grobmaschigere Gewebe werden als Sichtblende zwischen den Sälen und den entlanglaufenden Galerien eingesetzt. Sie filtern die Wahrnehmung des dahinter liegenden Raumes und lösen ihn in Farbpunkte auf. Personen können nur schemenhaft wahrgenommen werden.

Der Standort der Bibliothek ist für die zukünftige Entwicklung der Stadt von großer Bedeutung. Es handelt sich um eines der wenigen Gebiete inerhalb des Ringboulevards von Paris, wo auf größerer Fläche noch Platz ist für den Bau eines ganzen Stadtquartiers. In der Tradition der großen Stadterweiterungen entlang der Seine soll auch dieses Gebiet ›Seine Rive Gauche‹, das die Bibliothek umgibt, von Grund auf neu entstehen. Hierfür wurde die Entwicklungsgesellschaft Semapa gegründet, an der die Stadt mehrheitlich beteiligt ist. Die Gleisanlagen des Güterbahnhofs Tolbiac sind völlig verschwunden. Die Gleise des Gare d'Austerlitz, die das gesamte Gebiet durchziehen, werden in einer späteren Phase überbaut. Auf dem umgebenden Gebiet entsteht eine durch Blickachsen gegliederte Rasterstruktur mit Wohn- und Bürogebäuden. Der alte Bahnhof soll umgebaut werden. Dabei ist die Planung einer Schnellstraße weiterhin umstritten, die über den Gleisen durch die alte Bahnhofshalle führen soll.

Auf der gegenüberliegenden Seite der Seine entstand in den vergangenen Jahren unabhängig von der Bibliothek auf dem ehemaligen Areal des zentralen Weindepots der Stadt das Neubauquartier Bercy. Nach Fertigstellung einer Fußgängerbrücke über den Fluß wird dieses neue Quartier in wenigen Minuten von der Esplanade der Bibliothek aus zu erreichen sein. Damit wird dieser Stadtteil mit großem, liebevoll gestaltetem Park, 1200 Wohnungen und dem American Center von Frank O. Gehry als Blickpunkt von besonderer Bedeutung für die Benutzer der Bibliothek (vgl. S. 98 ff.). Strenge Richtlinien eines städtebaulichen Konzepts sorgen für eine homogene, in den Fassaden jedoch differenzierte und aufgelockerte Gestaltung. Für die einzelnen Blocks wurden so bedeutende Architekten wie Christian de Portzamparc, Yves Lion und Henri Ciriani beauftragt.

S.R.

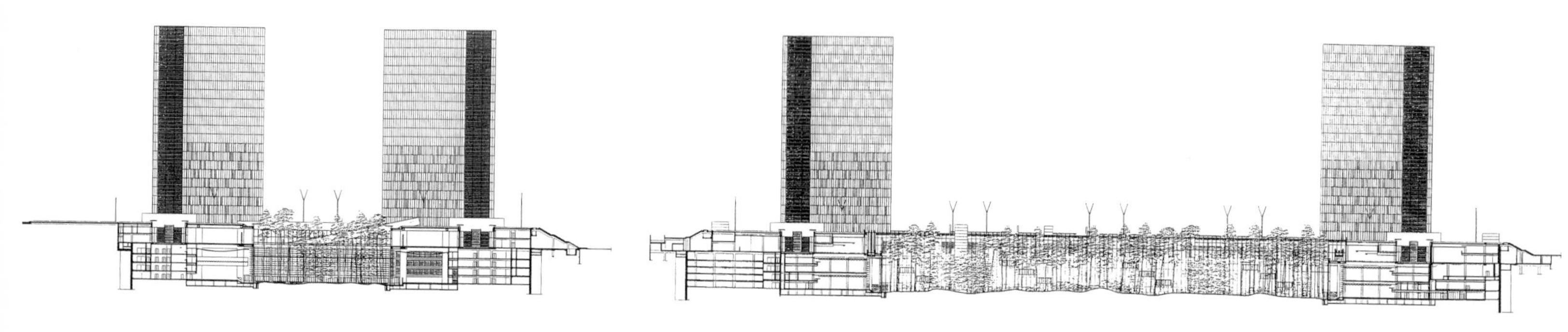

Der zentrale Hof der Bibliothek wird auf zwei Geschossen von einem breiten Erschließungsgang und den Lesesälen umgeben. 120 Kiefern, bis zu 20 Meter hoch, wurden mit großem Aufwand von der Normandie hierher verpflanzt. Die einzelnen Türme sind aufgeteilt in einen unteren Teil mit der Verwaltung und einen oberen 13geschossigen Teil mit den Buchmagazinen, die hinter hölzernen Trennwänden verborgen liegen.

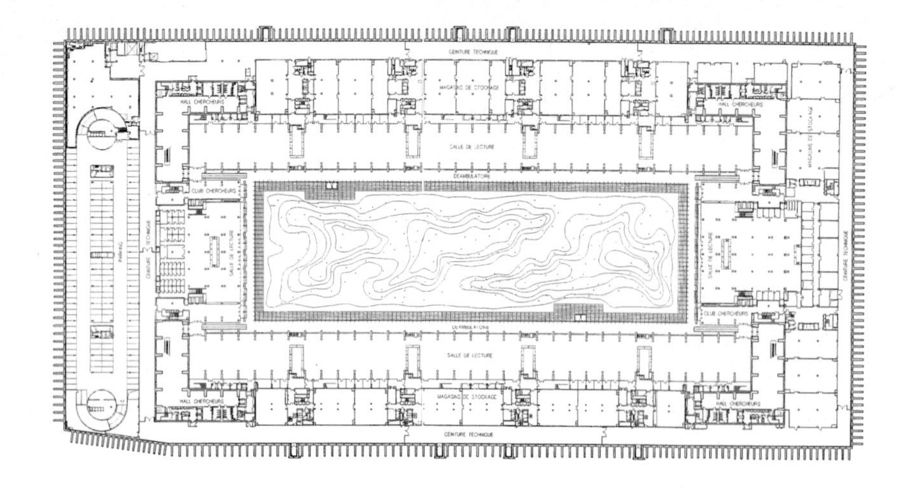

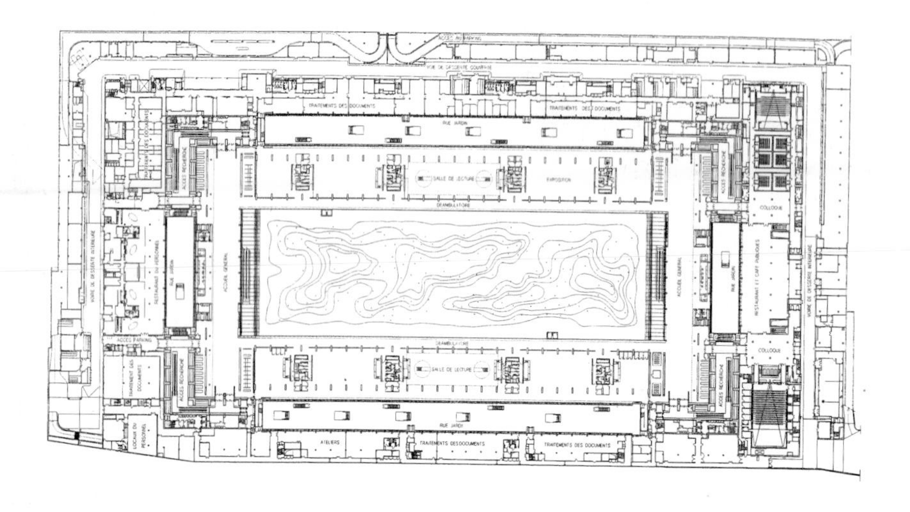

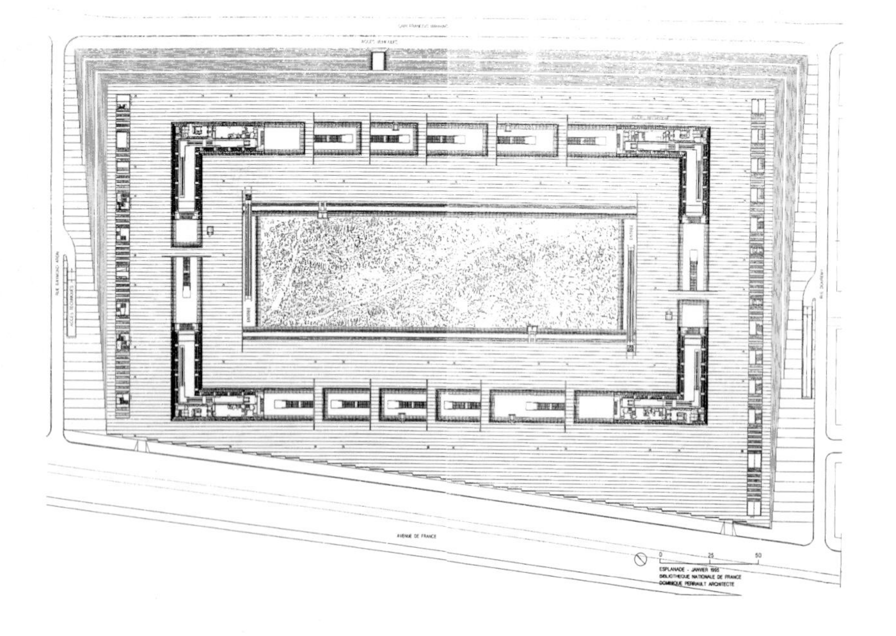

Die Grundrisse zeigen die obere Plattformebene mit den vier Türmen und die beiden Untergeschosse mit den Lesesälen. Im äußeren Ring verlaufen die Schienen des automatischen Buchverteilsystems ›Télédoc‹. Die untere Leseebene ist Forschern vorbehalten. Um dorthin zu gelangen, passieren die Besucher einen 30 Meter hohen, beängstigend wirkenden Erschließungsraum mit der Rolltreppe (Abbildung rechts).

Die Foyerzone wie auch die Lesesäle sind großzügig bemessen. Farblich bestimmend sind der Teppich in einem warmen Rot und die unterschiedlich abgehängten Stahlmatten, die die Decken verkleiden. Die große Höhe des unteren Lesesaals wurde genutzt, um weitere Lesekabinen brückenartig einzufügen (Abbildung rechts).

La Villette

Scientific Centre and Géode
Adrien Fainsilber
Reconstruction of the former slaughterhouse: Bernard Reichen, Philippe Robert
Halle Le Zénith: Philippe Chaix, Jean-Paul Morel

Parc de la Villette
Bernard Tschumi

Cité de la Musique
Christian de Portzamparc

Competition 1980
Constructed 1982–95

The planning of La Villette began in 1979. The site, which covers 35 hectares and was once occupied by the large slaughterhouses of Paris, is situated in the north-east of the city between Porte de Pantin and Porte de la Villette, or almost on the boundary with Aubervilliers. Initiated by President Valéry Giscard d'Estaing, this project was originally centred on the founding of a scientific centre, the National Museum for Science, Technology, and Industry. Its purpose was to promote a better understanding of scientific achievements and illustrate the effect on our lives of an increasingly technicized world.

The museum, which measures 275 × 111 × 40 metres, is four times the size of the Centre Pompidou and the biggest of its kind in the world. A country of technology devotees and enthusiasts, France has here created, symbolically as well, a place dedicated to information.

The architect Adrien Fainsilber, winner of the 1980 competition, did not build a museum in the classical sense but a 'Cité', a forum with open and transparent halls. The visitor is encouraged to participate by asking questions and conducting experiments with the aid of various computer terminals and projection screens. The permanent exhibition is aptly entitled 'Exploratorium', and the exhibits, which are displayed on six levels around the central atrium, range from submarines to space rockets, for example, one stage of the 'Ariane' launch vehicle. The exhibition's constituent sectors are technology, industrial production, information, and communication, its primary purpose being to convey a global understanding of technology and science and to show where disciplines overlap and interconnect. Each sector of the exhibition is updated or changed once a year.

The dimensions of the huge block were preordained, because the site was occupied by the unfinished shell of a new meat market. Planned under Charles de Gaulle and acclaimed as 'the abattoir of the year 2000', this had stood derelict for years. It had become unprofitable and redundant because refrigeration techniques had decentralized the slaughtering of cattle and transferred it to the country.

The present science centre is thus composed of the five bays originally intended for the abattoir, each of them supported by four massive columns. But for this existing shell, the museum would undoubtedly have been smaller and less costly. The installation of display areas entailed substantial alterations to the load-bearing structure. The building was invested with a 'castellar' dignity appropriate to its new function by surrounding it with wide moats, and the excavations provide the two exhibition levels situated below park-level with sufficient daylight. Superimposed on the building's long sides are huge, vivid blue lattice girders 8 metres high and 65 metres long. Seen from a distance, these are suggestive of an aircraft hangar. In the south, overlooking an expanse of water immediately outside, the building terminates in a conservatory 32 metres square. Likened to 'a transparent wrapper', this exceptionally light, self-supporting glass structure is a novel development and caused a great stir when completed.

The park that adjoins the museum in the east was designed by the Swiss architect Bernard Tschumi. Serving as a public recreation area and directly related to the museum by its 'paths of exploration', the park is transected by the Canal de l'Ourcq. The architect intended the area to be almost entirely covered by a regular pattern of pavilions 120 metres apart, 25 of which have been built and are thus situated in a system of coordinates. These bright red buildings, each of which has three floors and is 10 metres square, differ considerably. Many take the form of open frameworks, others are completely enclosed. Their functional significance also varies. They house a cinema, a café, a restaurant, an information centre, a children's play-house, studios, and sports facilities. Many serve merely as belvederes or bridge towers spanning the canal. The pavilions were originally intended to be restructured as required, being built on a modular system. Even for the competition, the architect called them 'folies' after the pleasure pavilions of the 18th century. Despite their dimensions, which are modest compared to those of the science centre, they soon became the park's unique trademark. They lend the huge suburban area the appearance of a coherent, readily identifiable ensemble.

The big expanses of grass are popular with sunbathers, expecially at weekends. The park is divided up by walkways. In the west, a three-kilometre promenade surmounted by a boldly undulating metal roof construction forms the shortest route between Porte de Pantin and Porte de la Villette. Winding paths traverse the various zones, some of which are already covered in dense vegetation. Situated in the midst of a sunken bamboo garden is the 'Cylindre sonore', a cylindrical resonating chamber open to the sky and used for acoustic experiments. Other areas are set off by fountains or sculptures, and the playground is dominated by a huge, horned dragon. By dissecting the expanse in this way, Tschumi has, in his own words, created the concept of an experiential world of 'balance and disorder'.

Seemingly afloat on a square pool in front of the 'Cité' is another of the park's features: the unique 'Géode', a futuristic-looking metal sphere with a diameter of 36 metres and a shiny outer skin. Concealed beneath the latter, which consists of 6433 triangular, slightly curved sheets of metal, is the spherical projection screen of an 'omnimax' cinema in which visitors can be launched into space or transported to the ocean floor.

Further to the south stands the former cattle hall of the slaughterhouse designed by Jules de Mérindol and dating from 1867. The architects Reichen + Robert have converted this important example of elegant 19th-century ironwork architecture into a 'Grande Halle' for public functions attended by as many as 15,000 people. In the north-east stands Philippe Chaix's and Jean-Paul Morel's 'Le Zénith', a hall 80 metres square used mainly for rock concerts. The thin plastic skin that conceals its plain, tubular steel structure is already looking rather the worse for wear.

The last buildings to be completed at La Villette were those of the Cité de la Musique, which was designed to relieve the pressure on the Conservatoire de Musique in Rue de Madrid, founded in 1911 by Gabriel Fauré. Described as 'a little music town' by its architect, Christian de Portzamparc, it clearly differs in architectural idiom from the other buildings and is divided into two areas. The first part is situated on the south-west edge of the park and houses the national academy of music and dance. In occupation since 1990, this contains lecture, rehearsal and recital rooms, a mediatheque and music library, and several apartments for the temporary accommodation of guests and teachers. The main building is surmounted by a strongly undulating, seemingly airborne roof that projects in some places and is pierced by a large oval aperture. The complex also embodies another range of buildings and underground recital rooms. The architect designed the roofs of the various halls as sculptural elements. A big flight of steps leads down to the sunken inner courtyard on to which the halls look out. Subdivided into four blocks, the slightly concave second range of buildings is separated from the busy Avenue Jean-Jaurès by the rehearsal rooms.

The central feature of the big concert hall that was opened two years ago – the stamping-ground of Pierre Boulez, who also made an active contribution to its planning – is a 'musical street' that spirals around the oval midpoint in the form of a covered, steadily tapering passage. The hall can hold anywhere between 800 and 1200 concert-goers, and the orchestra can be located in a variety of frontal or central positions. One special feature of the hall is the coloured lighting in the acoustic niches that run round it at balcony level. Flanking the 'street' are various facilities grouped in small blocks and integrated only by the uniform height of the eaves. Like the conservatoire, the concert hall is made up of a combination of diverse structural elements. The 'street', which also serves as a foyer, is transected at roof-level by a tapering lattice girder that projects into the entire structural complex. This, quite clearly, is Portzamparc's daring contribution to the architectural deconstructivism current throughout Europe during the planning phase. Situated beneath the girder is the diagonal axis that cuts across the 'musical street' and marks the main entrance. The metal structure surmounting this is designed to take account of Tschumi's pattern of red 'folies'.

Portzamparc's strongly sculptural and 'fragmentary' idiom is in clear contrast to the other buildings at La Villette, notably Aldo Rossi's adjoining apartment block, and lends expression to their special function.

La Villette has been generally well received by the local population. Traversed during the day by parties of schoolchildren and filled with activity at night by those who attend its various public functions, it is now, at weekends, one of the French capital's foremost public parks.

S.R.

The National Museum for Science, Technology, and Industry is the biggest of its kind in the world. The gigantic metal sphere, the "Géode", with a diameter of 36 metres, houses a cinema seating 370 and a huge, concave screen.

Following pages
The 35 hectare park was designed by Bernard Tschumi. The three-storeyed, red "folies" or pavilions, which all differ in appearance, have been constructed in a system of coordinates. To date, 25 have been completed.

LA LUMIERE DEMASQUEE
ESPACE DIDEROT

CROIXEMENT!
information VILLETTE
information VILLETTE

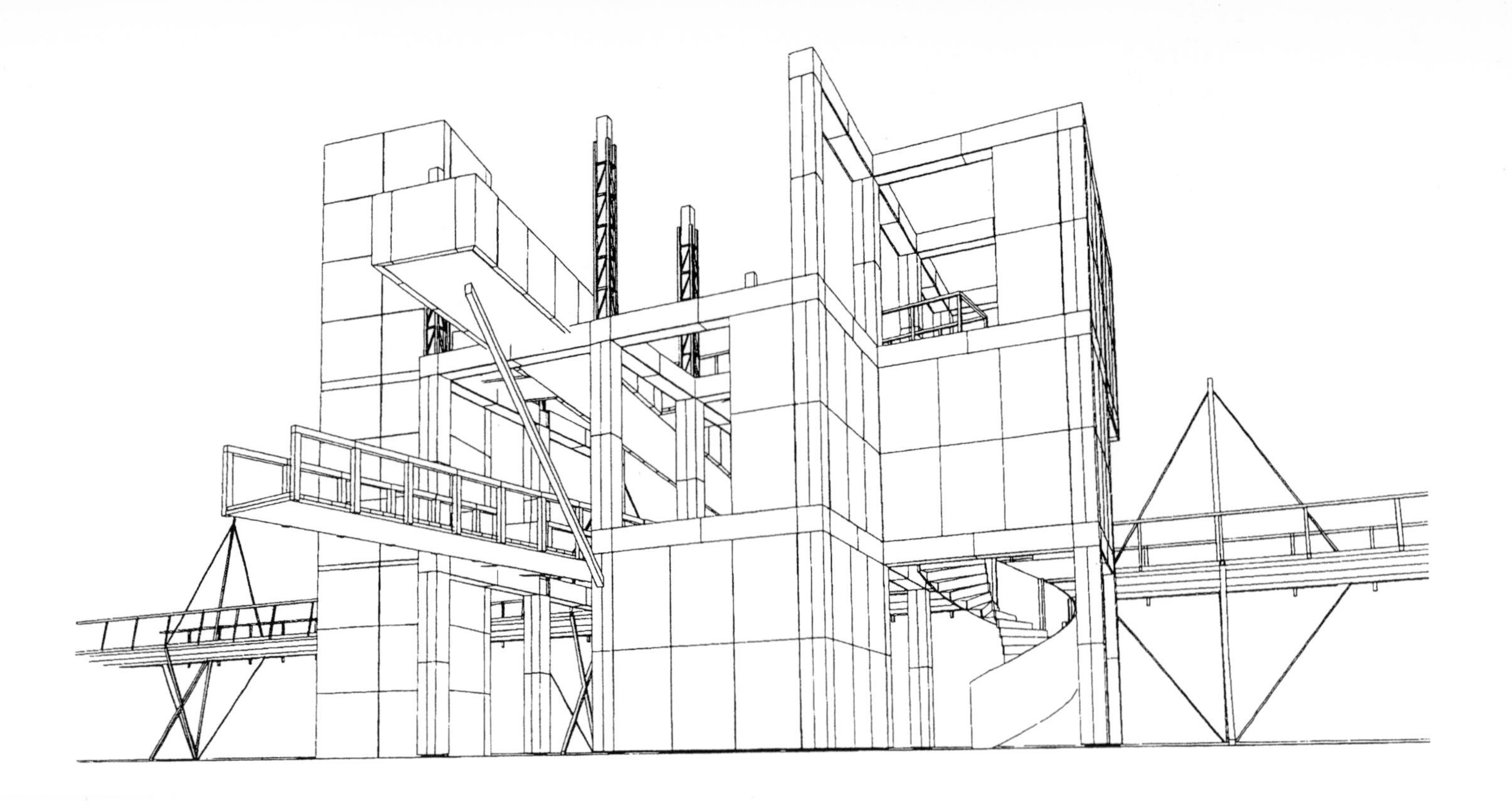

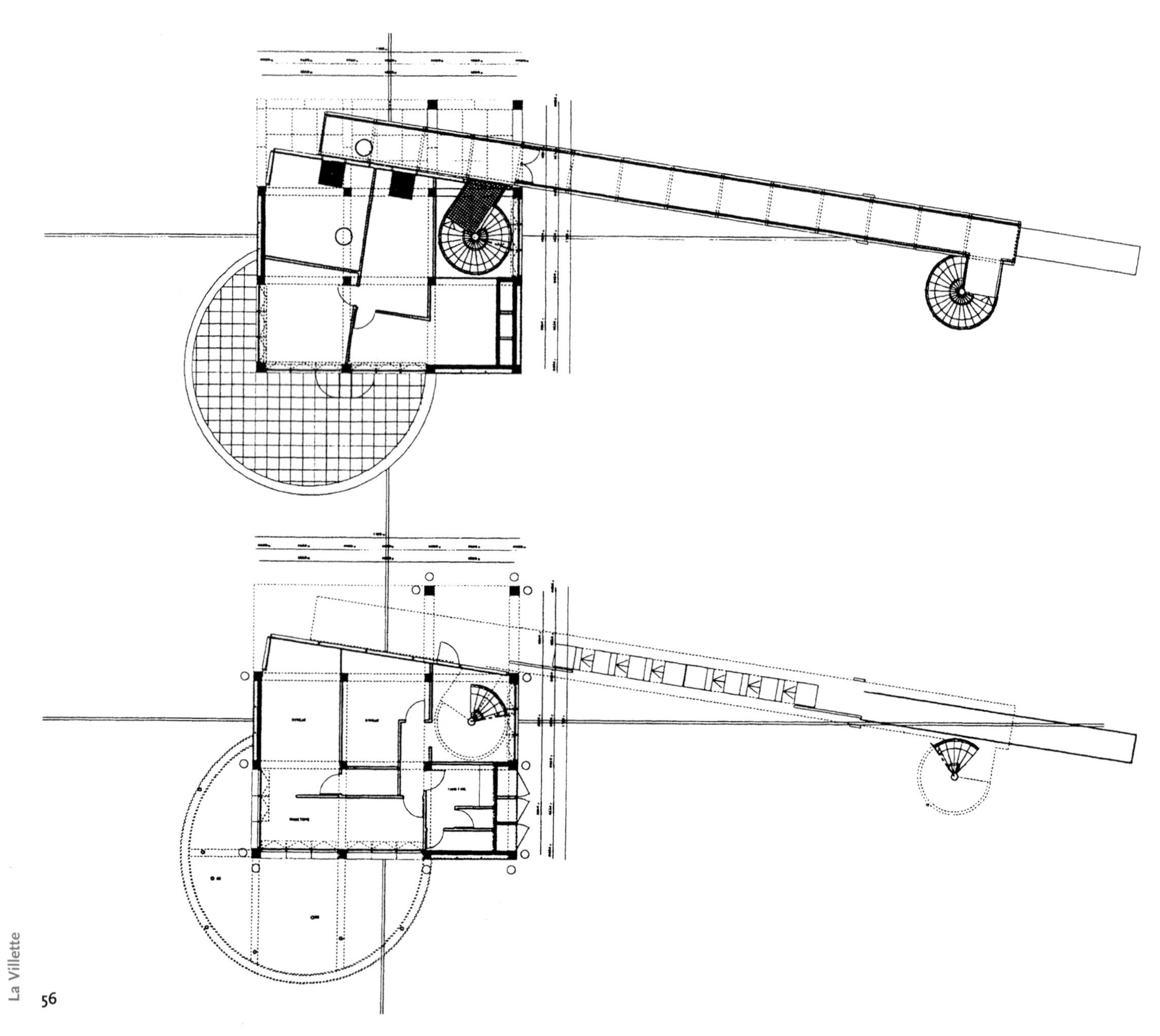

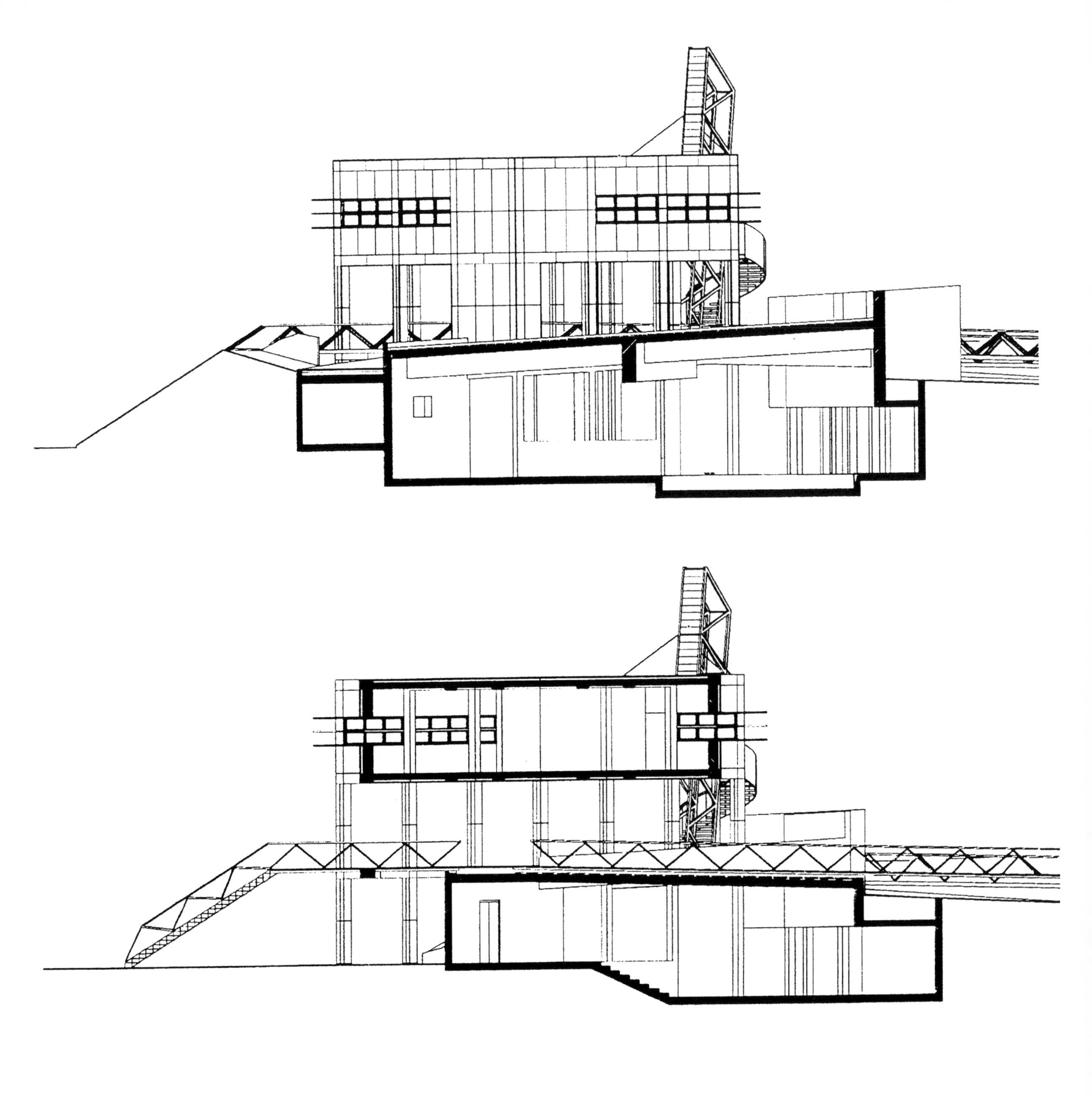

Floor plans, cross-sections and elevations of the
pavilions which are used for a variety of functions.
These include a bar, exhibition area, shops, information office, etc.
Some of the "folies" are linked by walkways.

Each "folie" has its own function and distinctive architecture. La Villette has become the largest urban park in Paris and is now a recreation area popular with both those living in the city centre as well as those from the suburbs.

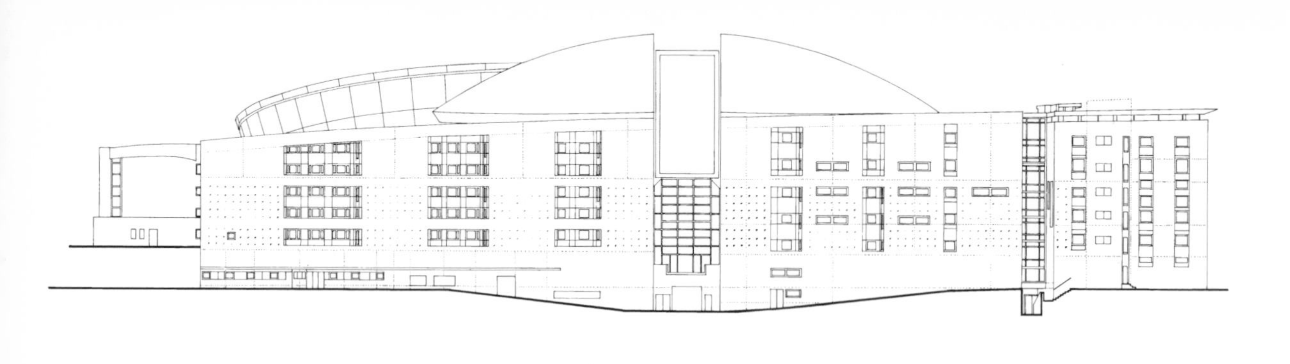

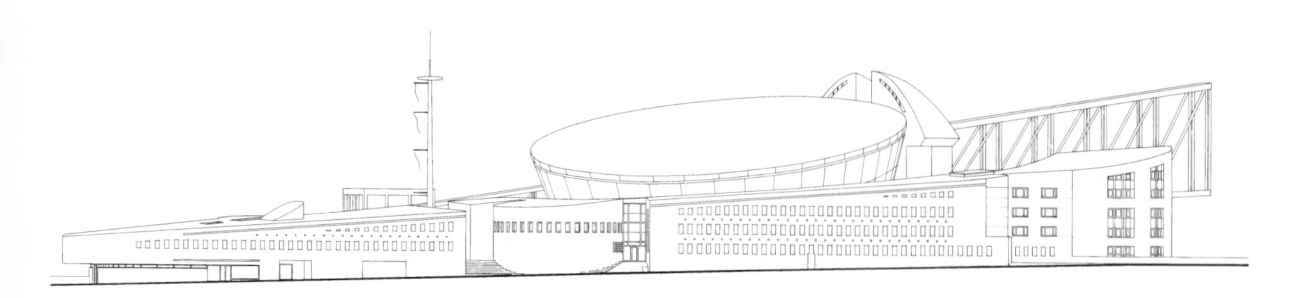

The last buildings to be completed were those at the southern tip of the park, which form the extensive Cité de la Musique, designed by Christian de Portzamparc. The large oval hall is surrounded by a music museum, administrative offices, student housing, a café and a police station.

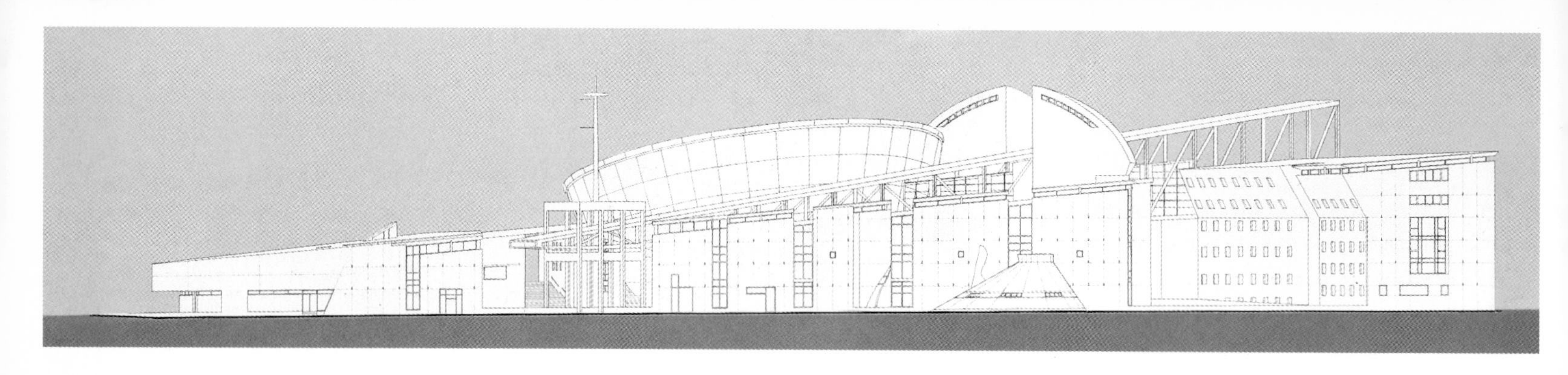

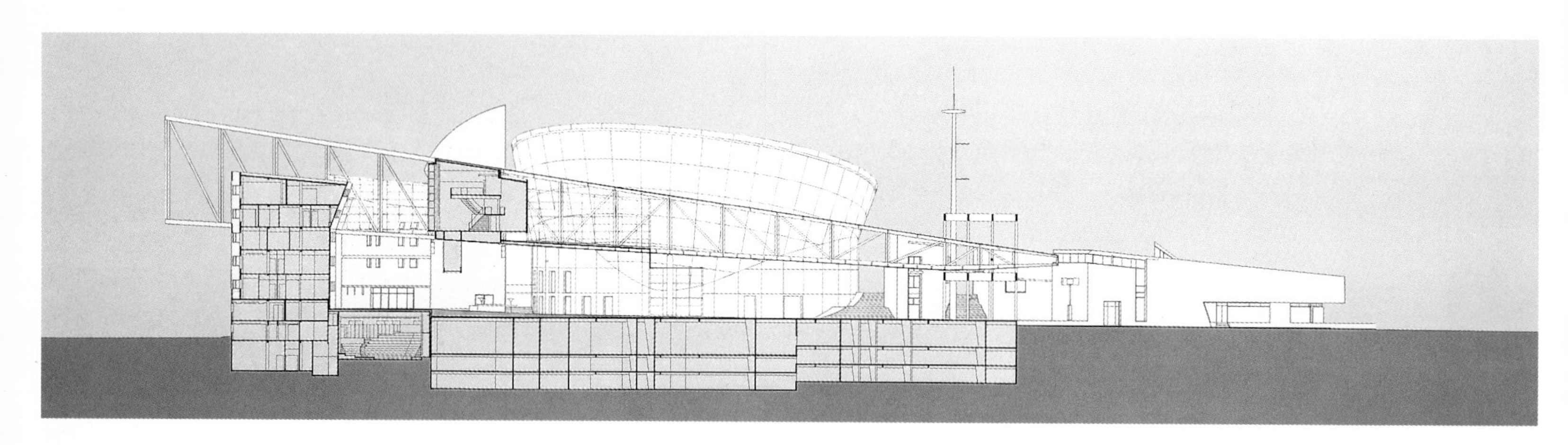

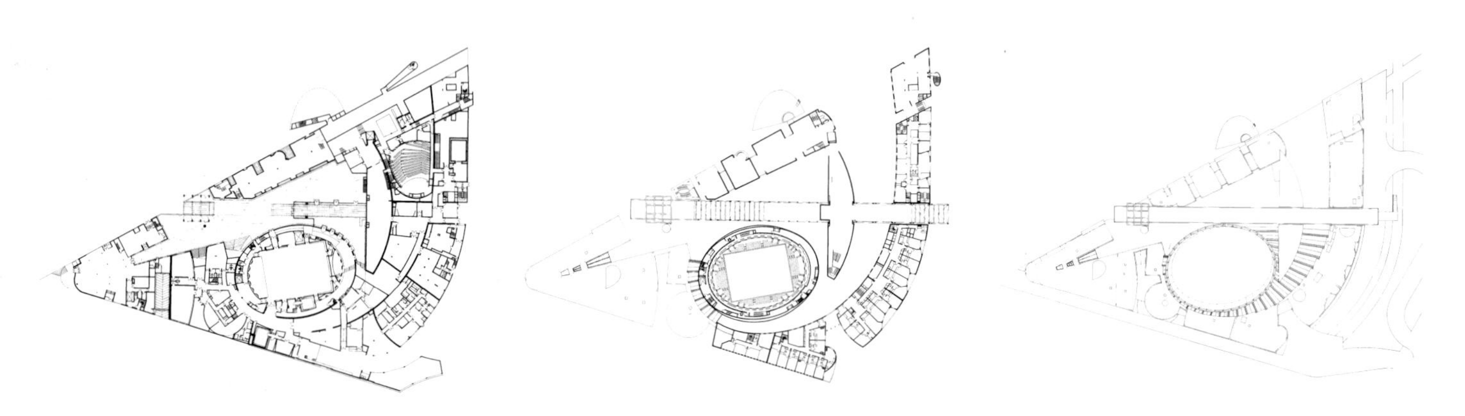

Floor plans and cross-sections of the Cité de la Musique.

The central element of the "music town" is a "musical street" – a covered passageway that winds its way around a central hall. A massive girder, thrust through the building complex, marks the entrance at the southern gate of the park. The support is in line with Bernard Tschumi's system of coordinates used to align the pavilions.

The following double page shows the large concert hall, which seats 1200. The flexible design means that the orchestra can be accommodated either at the front or centrally. The oval hall is the "home ground" of Pierre Boulez.

The first phase of the Cité de la Musique was opened in 1990 and houses the national academy of music and dance as well as lecture theatres, practice rooms, and accommodation for dancers and musicians. The building was also designed by Christian de Portzamparc.

Views of the spacious foyer areas.
The roofs of the various halls have, in part, been designed as sculptural architectural elements.
The main building is characterized by the large undulating roof.

Muséum National d'Histoire Naturelle

Paul Chemetov, Borja Huidobro

Competition 1987
Constructed 1992–5

The natural history museum in the Jardin des Plantes, a venerable institution founded in 1626, in the reign of Louis XIII, was long overshadowed by the big museums of Paris. Selected by President Mitterrand to be one of the last 'Grands Projets de l'Etat' – a choice that surprised many people – the museum's Grande Galerie was reopened in June 1994, after an interval of 30 years. The Musée de l'Histoire Naturelle had been inaugurated as the world's first zoological museum in 1889, the same year as the Eiffel Tower. The architect Jules-Louis André (1819–90), a pupil of Henri Labrouste, had decided on a internal structure which, though daring in design, was not discernible from outside: two encircling galleries and a big glass roof supported by slender cast-iron columns. The building had to be closed in the 1960s because of structural damage.

In 1987 a competition for architects and scenographers was won by Paul Chemetov and Borja Huidobro of Paris in collaboration with the stage designer René Allio. The team of architects had earned a name for themselves with the new, recently completed building for the Ministry of Finance, situated only a few hundred metres from the museum.

The reconstruction of the Grande Galerie de Zoologie is based on a novel conception for the entire museum. Not restricted to the displaying of stuffed animals and skeletons, this aims to encourage visitors to reflect on the relationship between the human race and nature as a whole. The architects supplemented the structure of the central hall with steel-and-glass installations characterized by cool restraint and a great attention to detail; a deliberate attempt to 'alienate' the visitor from the animals displayed in motion. These installations are entirely devoid of illusionistic effects, their aim being to preclude any impression that the animals are alive and located in their natural environment.

To create more room for temporary exhibitions and public functions, the museum was enlarged in a downwards direction by excavating the soil beneath the hall to a depth of ten metres. The masonry foundations were left exposed and laterally bounded by concrete and steel frames. The newly created premises were roofed over with a concrete platform corresponding in height to the hall's original floor. Unlike those of the art museum into which the Gare d'Orsay was converted, its original dimensions have fortunately been preserved. The platform, which can only be reached by way of glass bridges, is reserved for land animals. The denizens of the savannah – elephants and giraffes, zebras and rhinoceroses – troop across the spacious hall in a serried, lifelike procession. The area devoted to creatures of the desert is bathed in warm yellow artificial light. Along the sides of the hall, other species of animals are displayed in smaller exhibition areas and tall, glass-fronted cabinets. Cold white light characterizes another environment: here, polar bears repose on slanting sheets of frosted glass that take the place of ice-floes.

Many specimens in this collection are very old. The rhinoceros, for example, came to France in 1770 and spent many decades in the royal menagerie at Versailles.

At the sides of the platform are spacious recesses from which visitors can look down into the new basement. Fitted into this open space on one of the hall's long sides are the glass lift and the stairs. Located on the other side are huge whale skeletons that illustrate the transition of life forms from land to sea. Birds hover above, near the lift, whereas fish and marine mammals are displayed below the platform.

It is fascinating to observe the ingenious way in which lighting has been used to distinguish the various environments. Each group of creatures is illuminated in a colour of its own, and additional, variable, lighting issues from an 'active glass roof'. Within the space of one hour and forty minutes, visitors experience an entire day in time-lapse. The big glass roof of the central hall, originally intended to dispense natural light, was converted so as to produce artificial lighting effects: a bright blue summer sky turns stormy grey and ultimately transforms itself into a blood-red sunset. This changing light is accompanied by a sound installation.

The upper gallery informs visitors about the history and theory of evolution. The final part of this exhibition area is devoted to a graphic depiction of the consequences of

The radical remodelling of the museum, situated in the Jardin des Plantes, resulted in an enlargement downwards by excavating beneath the hall to a depth of ten metres. This has created more space for temporary exhibitions and new rooms for a variety of uses.

human interference with nature. The effects of agriculture and hunting are shown, as are those of environmental pollution and urban development. The museum's long east wing has been left as it was. The stuffed animals reside in old, beautifully crafted display cabinets.

The redesigning of this natural history museum's central hall has not only put a novel scientific concept into effect but brilliantly restored and reconstructed an historical monument.

The extinction of species continues unabated. In the last ten years, for instance, the African elephant population has halved, and the beasts are already threatened with annihilation in many parts of the East African savannah by the illicit trade in their magnificent ivory tusks. Today, therefore, it is the vital and overriding task of natural history museums to mount exhibitions designed to convince people of the importance of wild-life conservation.

S.R.

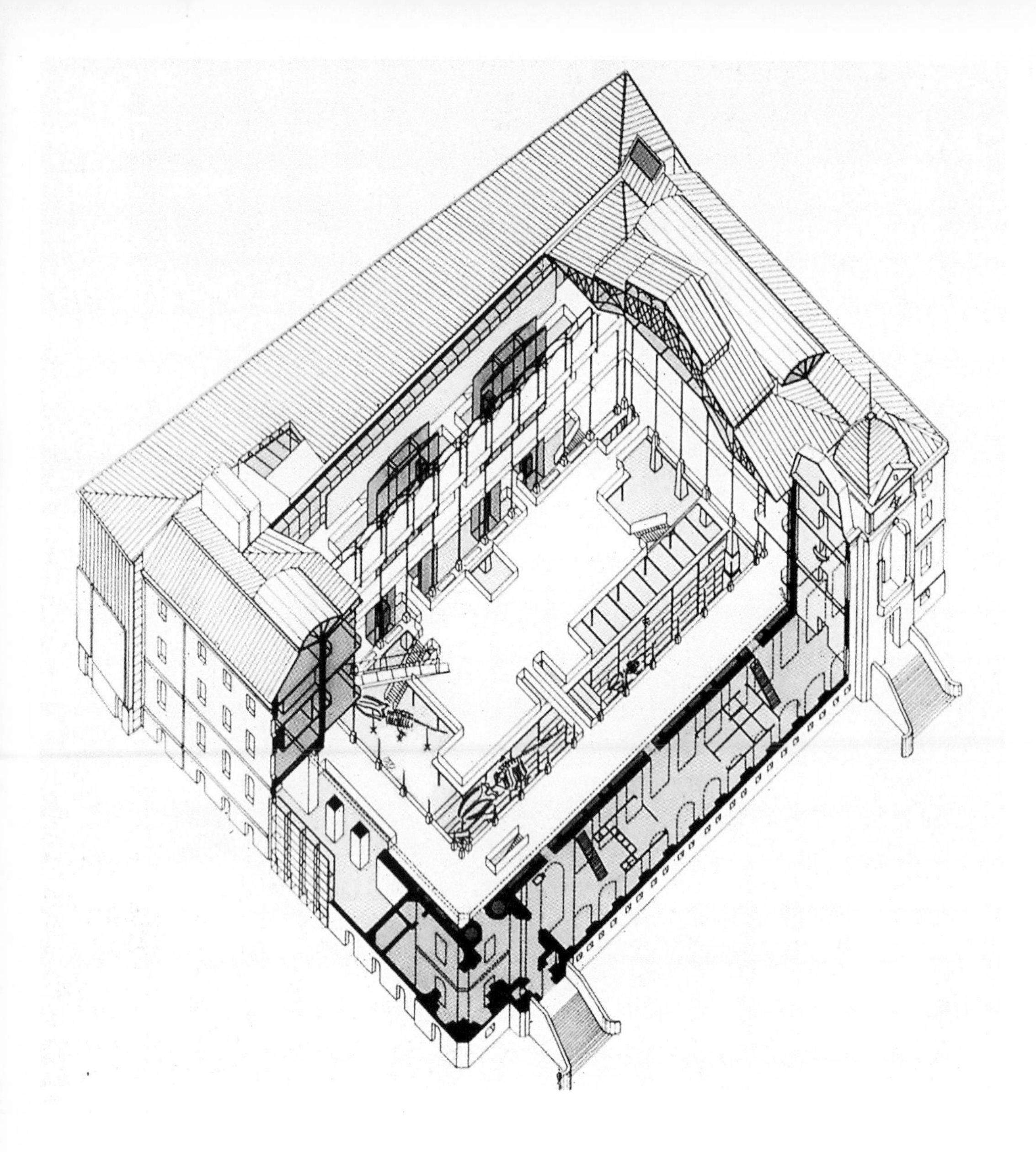

This sectional view and the cross-section clearly show the museum's expansion below ground level and the completely reinstated central hall which, with its parade of animals of the savannah, elephants and giraffes, zebras and rhinoceroses trooping through the building in tight formation, still forms the museum's focal point. Small exhibition areas have now been created around the sides.

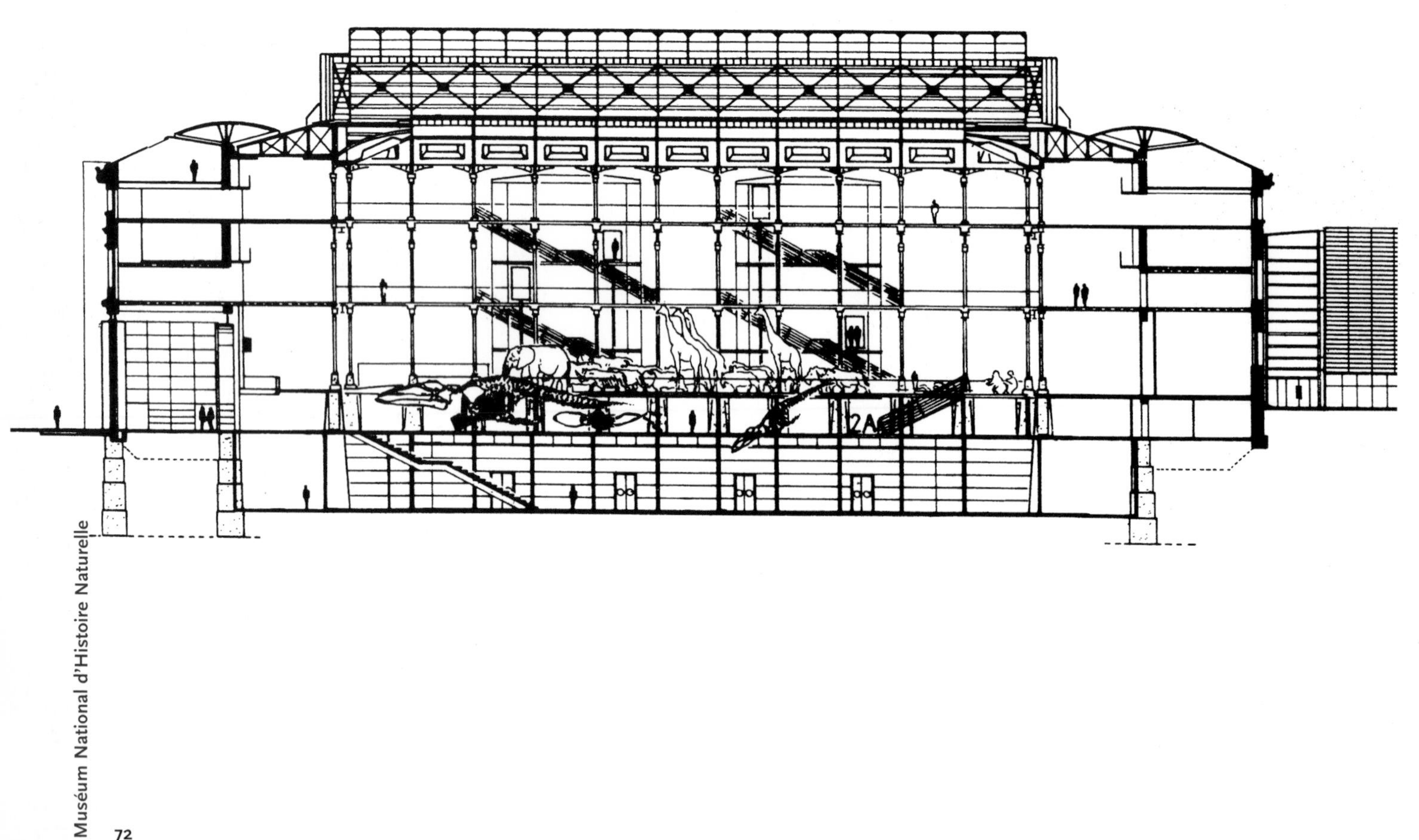

Views of the central hall with the principal section of stuffed animals (top), the completely redesigned entrance area (centre), and the exhibition space on the lower level (bottom). This newly created space below the central hall accommodates, among other exhibits, a comprehensive collection of fish (facing page).

Fondation Cartier

Jean Nouvel, Emmanuel Cattani

Completion 1994

Cartier is part of Paris. In Montparnasse, just before Boulevard Raspail runs into the Place Denfert-Rochereau, stands a new and striking building owned by the exclusive, worldwide concern. Its volume and structure are not immediately apparent. The first thing passers-by see is a glass frontage, eight metres high, that conforms to the building line. They are then surprised to discover that behind it lies, not a building, but a garden containing some pollarded chestnut trees – a kind of terrarium open to the sky. The free-standing wall of clear glass becomes a window displaying an artificial landscape of vague extent.

The building itself is twice as high and set back twelve metres from the street. Its true outlines become discernible only on closer inspection, since its façade is wider and higher than its actual volume. The free-standing lateral façades are also glazed and run the full height of the building.

Cartier, the fashionable Parisian jewellery house established in 1847, decided to entrust its glass palace to the architects Jean Nouvel and Emmanuel Cattani, who had previously built it two workshops in Switzerland. Accommodated in the Boulevard Raspail building are exhibition rooms for Cartier's modern art foundation, now ten years old, and, on the upper floors, its main administrative offices. Cartier boss Alain Dominique Perrin, an enthusiastic art collector, is keen to provide a forum for young French and foreign artists.

The design was partly determined by an old tree with historical associations. The cedar of Lebanon that flanks the boulevard on a level with the centre of the site is said to have been planted at the beginning of the 19th century by Chateaubriand. The new building was also to be set back from the street. This accounts for the unusual idea of an intermediate area containing a garden enclosed by sheets of glass and affording a view of the exhibition rooms. The only opening in the glass wall is the entrance, and a paved path leads into the building beneath the cedar's massive umbrella. Seen through the numerous glass walls, outlines become blurred. Reflections, images of real and virtual trees, the art installations in the background, the transformation of sheets of glass into projection screens – all these help to create a fascinating visual puzzle. Brightly illuminated at night, Cartier's new home plays still more optical tricks that manifest the full extent of the mysterious, sometimes bizarre interaction between the material and the immaterial.

Once inside, visitors are confronted on the ground floor by an almost entirely glassed-in exhibition hall. Nouvel describes this area as an 'espace nomade' in which young artists can install their works with total freedom. Exhibitions are changed every three months.

Three square sheets of glass are let into the floor on the left of the entrance. These can be folded up to facilitate the emplacement of installations more than two storeys high and enable bulky works of art to be transported to the exhibition room in the basement.

The garden at the rear is accessible from the exhibition hall by way of room-high glass doors that can be slid outwards into the free-standing façades. This is where Perrin proposes to hold artistic happenings. Mature trees, some already *in situ* and others imported at great expanse, form a variegated backdrop in front of the wall that abuts the neighbouring properties.

Unlike the one on the ground floor, the exhibition room in the basement is only six metres high and windowless. The original intention was to construct a sunken sculpture courtyard at the rear on the lines of Mies van der Rohe's Neue Nationalgalerie in Berlin, but this plan was abandoned. The result is an introverted, whitewashed room whose only natural illumination derives from three glass lights in the ceiling. Beneath this exhibition room are another two floors containing storage space and workshops, as well as four parking levels. This means that the building has almost as many floors below ground as above. Cartier cars are parked by lift. Having been consigned to one of the two steel mesh parking boxes beside the main entrance, they are transported to their allotted spaces far below ground by means of a preprogrammed code. The top floor is well set back and affords a panoramic view of the city. This is the only place where wood was used. The firm's conference rooms and the terraces outside are fitted with wooden planks like on a ship's deck.

The building has no internal staircases or lifts. To reach the offices on the upper seven floors the exhibition area has to be crossed to reach one of the glass cabins at the rear, which glide silently up and down the façade. The steel stair-

In May 1994, the Cartier modern art foundation opened its new exhibition rooms at 261 Boulevard Raspail. The offices of the Cartier company are in the upper storeys. Jean Nouvel's design was conditioned by a tree – a Lebanese cedar, reputedly planted by Chateaubriand. This national monument forced him to set the building back 12 metres from the road.

ways, too, are outside and wholly exposed to the elements. Having dispensed with internal stairs so as to create more flexibly utilizable space, Nouvel compensated for this by installing an extra lift.

Nouvel's aim was to construct a building 'without design and details'. There are, in fact, no exciting high-tech accessories, and no superfluous fripperies can be discerned.

The office areas are characterized by elegant simplicity. Executed with great precision, the interior design is limited to a few materials employed with meticulous care. The grey-carpeted floors are structured with wide bands of aluminium that echo the framework of the building. The tables and cupboards, which were specially designed for Cartier by the architect himself, could hardly be less pretentious. His plans were centred not so much on efficient utilization in terms of business management but rather on creating a largely open structure and enhancing the firm's image.

Cartier has to spend a great deal on maintenance to keep its glass palace a Parisian jewel that glitters in the sunlight by day and scintillates at night.

S.R.

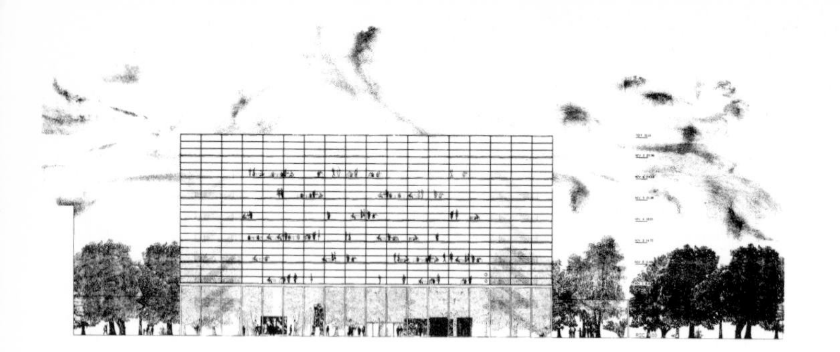

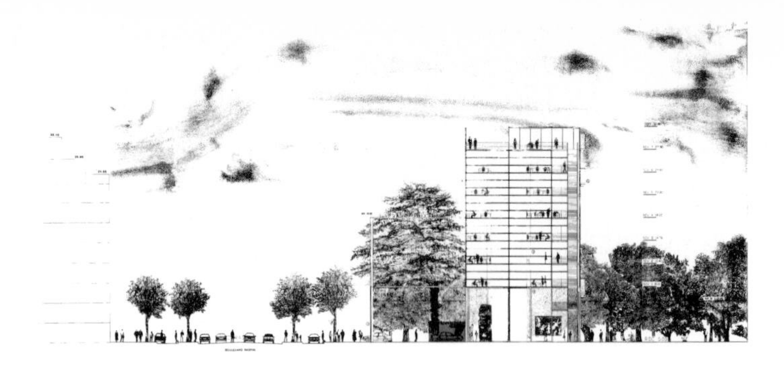

Floor plans, directors floor, offices and the exhibition space on the ground floor, as well as a cross-section.
The building has 8 storeys above ground and 7 below, 4 of which provide parking space. The stairs are outside against the freestanding façade.

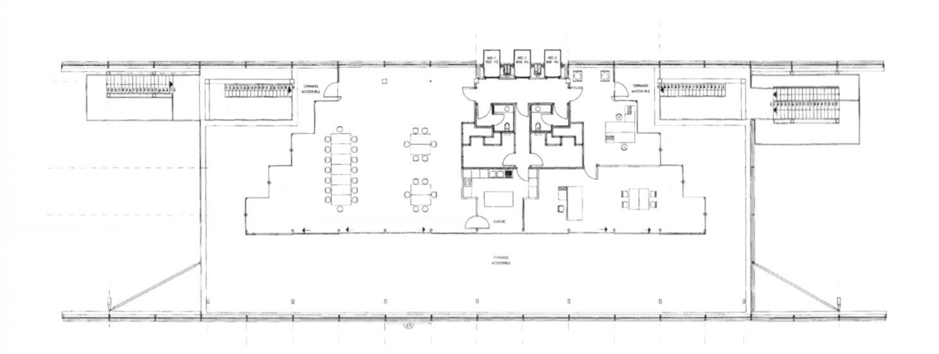

A glass façade in line with neighbouring buildings, screens the property from the street and distorts views. A fascinating kaleidoscope of images is caused by the reflection of light and mirrored images.

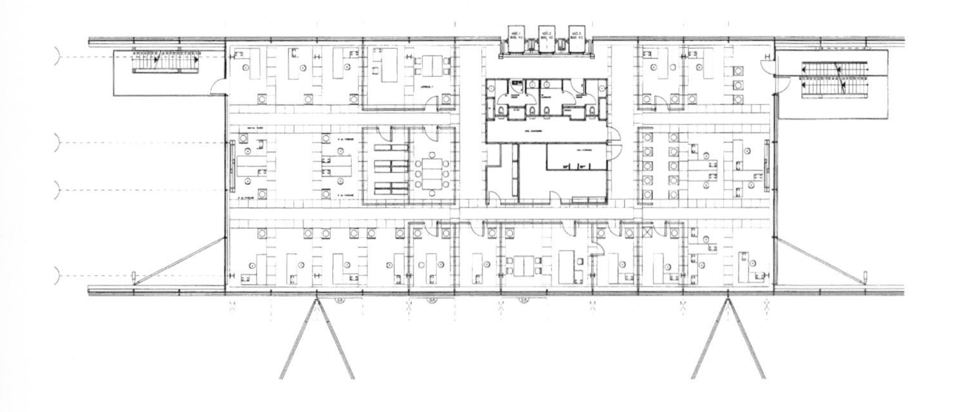

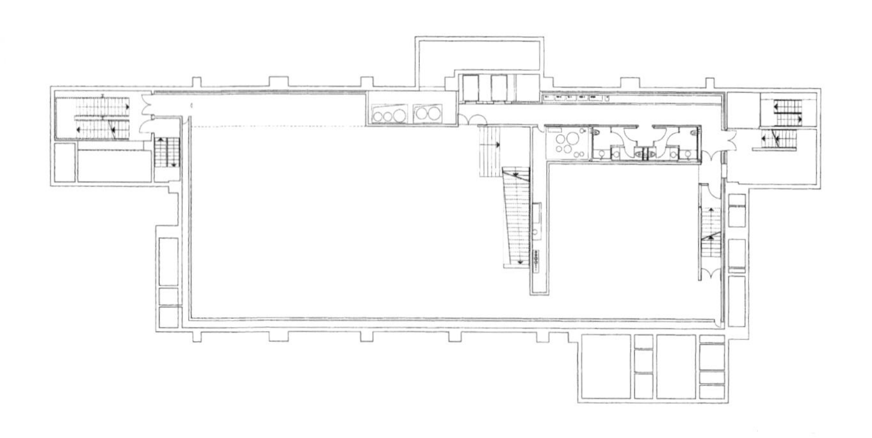

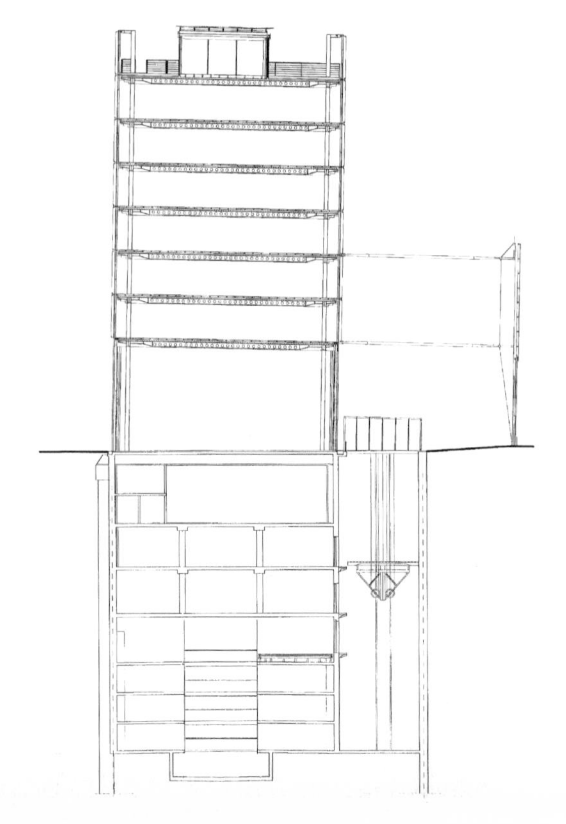

View from the directors' floor with roof terrace. Jean Nouvel also designed the furniture.

The exhibition hall on the ground floor is traversed by a narrow gallery at the entrance. The visitor crosses the room to reach the lifts which are against the rear façade.

The hall is used for temporary exhibitions. At its opening works by Richard Artschwager and Ron Arad were shown.

Théâtre National de la Colline

Alberto Cattani, Valentin Fabre, Jean Perrottet

Completion 1987

'All the world's a stage...' Perhaps, but architectural reality usually belies this statement. Ever since the Greeks of the 6th century B.C. not only sang and danced but 'played' in honour of Dionysus, and ever since Aeschylus or Sophocles founded the European performing arts, including opera, operetta and the dance, in semicircular hollows converted with a minimum of architectural intervention into public 'places for seeing' (the original meaning of the Greek word 'theatron'), latter-day theatres have seldom heeded the importance once attached to the public nature of such places. On the contrary: as the theatrical architecture of Greece and Rome developed, so theatres, formerly simple and inviting, became monumentalized into awe-inspiring cultural temples. All the world was no longer a stage; indeed, there was a growing tendency for the stage to exclude the rest of the world with the aid of an architecture that builds us sacrosanct halls and must bear architectonic responsibility for the oft-cited crisis in the theatre.

Quite the contrary applies to the Théâtre National de la Colline, which opened in Paris's 20th Arrondissement in October 1987. There in Rue Malte-Brun, a small side street in the east of the city, the Parisian architects Valentin Fabre and Jean Perrottet (in collaboration with Alberto Cattani) conjured the virtue of welcoming transparency out of the constraints of a cramped site once occupied by a cinema, bounded on three sides by fire walls, and only 16 metres wide where it abuts the street. The entrance hall, foyer and various accesses adjoin the street and lead up to the two auditoriums. The larger of the two and its stage occupy the full depth of the site, which covers 1700 square metres and can seat 770, whereas the smaller, versatile auditorium is designed to seat 250. Thus, almost the entire frontage itself gives the impression of a stage. Optically sustained by a massive ferroconcrete framework divided into square fields and splayed between the adjoining buildings, the glass wall presents an inviting, visually accessible theatre to the gaze of the district's strollers and idlers, shopkeepers and customers, residents and workers: a 'place for seeing' in the best (Greek) sense. People outside in the street can take in the whole of the theatre and its activities at a glance: the foyer, the gallery, and the full depth of the auditorium, the backs of whose graduated rows of seats intrude into the foyer. The designers (whose Théâtre de la Ville marked them as skilful theatrical architects back in the 1960s) have thus made the best of their inability to provide the theatre with an adequate forecourt: the street itself fulfils that function and transforms the place into a stage.

The result is a building that carries conviction on the stage and in the street alike. This is precisely because its claims to attention stem from thorough analysis of urban topography and scrupulous internal organization, not from any architectural bombast or stagey attempt to impress. And this, in turn, is why the theatre looks so remarkably fresh and innovative almost a decade after its opening. In other words, as the box office figures testify, it is perfectly qualified to play the 'jeune premier' of the locality.

The architects, when questioned about their professional philosophy: 'We always try to adopt a functional approach to our commissions.' That is why the theatre is not merely a place whose architectonic symbolism shines far out across a quarter ill provided with cultural centres, but a modern, going concern whose internal space has been skilfully utilized. To give access to the premises devoted to storage and set construction, the architects designed the glass façade like an outsize swing door. Pivoted inwards, it discloses a ramp that enables trucks to reach the offset stage directly from Rue Malte-Brun. Situated with equal simplicity above this engagingly simple combination of delivery bay, main entrance, façade and street theatre are the administrative offices.

The design of this unpretentious theatre, which contrasts so agreeably with 'theatrical' theatre architecture, is such as to lure inquisitive strollers and curious passers-by into the glass entrance hall that develops into the foyer, grows into the auditorium, and transforms itself into the stage. Here at least, though all the world may not be a stage, all the street is a theatre.

G.M.

Only a thin glass wall separates the foyer from the world outside in the Rue Malte-Brun, in the 20th Arrondissement. In the evening, the members of the audience themselves become actors in the brightly lit theatre entrance. A spiral staircase, visible from the street, links the two levels.

Walkways and galleries provide theatrical internal and external views between the viewing area and the functional side. The use of unpretentious materials such as concrete, steel and glass ensure they do not gain prominence.

To squeeze the theatre in an opening just 16 metres wide, the building stretches right back across the site. The asymmetrically constructed stages provide a space between the neighbouring buildings. Access to the offset stage can even be made by trucks via an outsized glass swing door.

NESCO
AISES

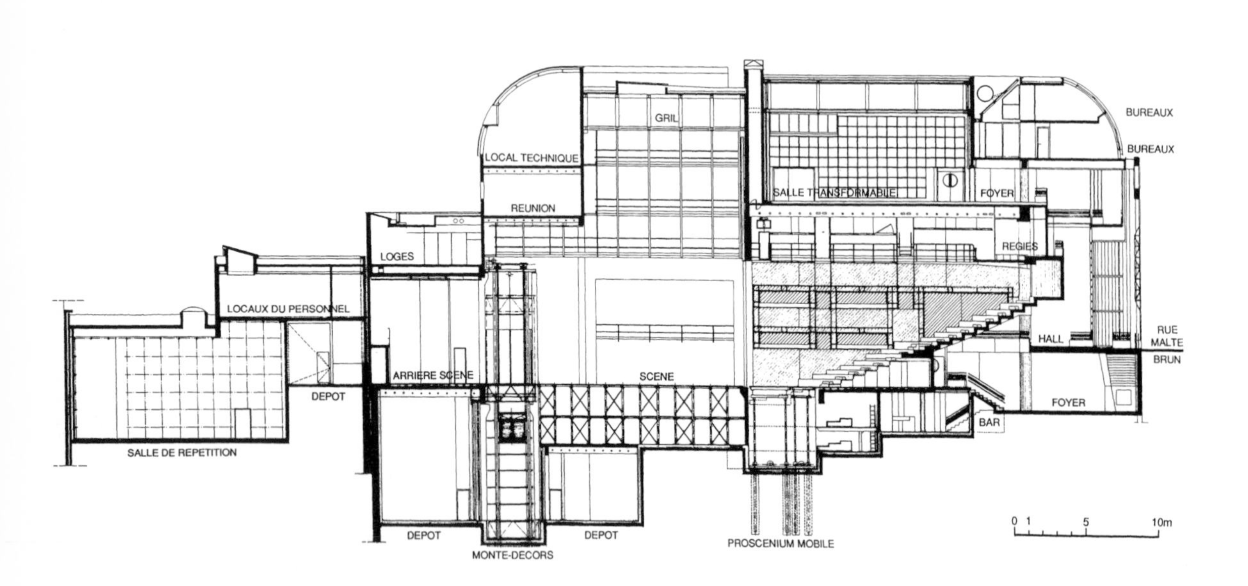

Steps lead down from the foyer at street level to the bar and the carefully furnished refreshments area which, despite being open, has an almost intimate atmosphere. The transparent glass façade is supported by a mighty reinforced concrete structure. The longitudinal section shows the cleverly arranged storage and equipment rooms behind and above the stage areas. The offices are situated above the foyer overlooking the road and with a good supply of natural light.

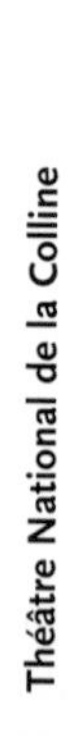

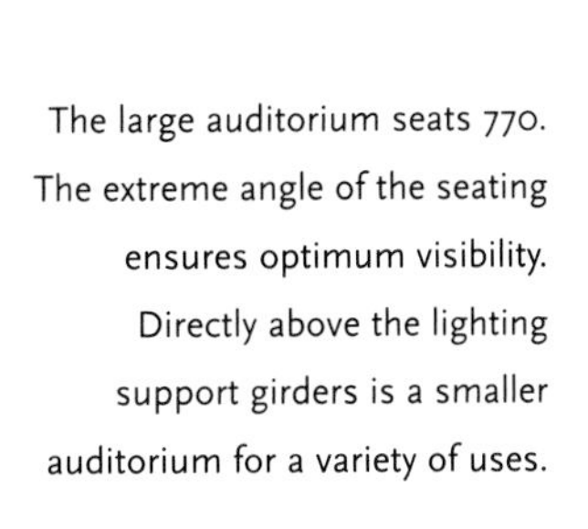

The large auditorium seats 770. The extreme angle of the seating ensures optimum visibility. Directly above the lighting support girders is a smaller auditorium for a variety of uses.

Canal+ Headquarters

Richard Meier

Completion 1992

'Its image from the Seine is of a great ship whose only movement is the changing light.' (Richard Meier)

It beams at us in all its celebrated, immaculate whiteness from the glossy pages of architectural magazines: the new headquarters of Canal Plus, the French commercial television network. This and his widely acclaimed town house in Ulm are two of Richard Meier's most recent works on the old continent. Hardly had it been completed when it was robbed of its artificial perfection. Swathed in huge nets designed to arrest the slabs of stone that fall from it with murderous unpredictability, the big building seems to be stranded on the northern edge of the Parc Citroën, thereby, with inadvertent irony, adding a new variant to architecture's stock of nautical metaphors. This, we are led to believe, is a purely structural problem that will be solved and consigned to the past, swiftly forgotten in view of an architectural design that has not only justified the fairest hopes but fulfilled great expectations.

Unlike Frank Gehry, who was personally commissioned to design the American Center, Richard Meier was chosen on the strength of a competition. And although the two American architects have little else in common, their projects are comparable in that both are situated in the immediate neighbourhood of two important new parks. They are also comparable in being located in one of those disparate settings – industrial estates, motorways, run-down residential districts – that Paris is spawning all along the Seine and has now declared 'Zones d'Aménagement Concerté' open to radical reconstruction.

The immediate environs of the plot between Rue Balard and Quai André Citroën are not particularly inspiring from the architectural point of view. A butterfly-shaped high-rise monster of the 1960s stands opposite and an equally desolate box of the same period bounds the site in the east, though the white-tiled semicircle of an Art Déco development invites closer scrutiny and encourages a fleeting dialogue. Although the site comprises an almost complete block, an underground long-distance telephone exchange reduced the scope for spatial development to a narrow, tapering, L-shaped area facing the Seine. Into this has been fitted the three- or four-part complex that provides the network's administrative, managerial and production teams with an impressive home. The offices face the Seine, the production premises the street. The link between the two is supplied by the multi-storey entrance hall and a corner building with a curving glass façade, which also contains offices. This arrangement not only seems sensible and comprehensible but can be detected in the formal treatment of individual volumes: largely secluded in the case of the studios, open and transparent in varying degrees where the other working and reception areas are concerned. The cinema looms over the entire complex like a truncated cone. The slender, cylindrical stairway towers, which are let into the corners like hinges, the flying roof that pays yet another tribute to Le Corbusier, the slightly convex segment in the east, and the concave glass membrane of the western corner – all these help to supplement and relieve the consistently rectangular geometry of the whole, though the east front of the office block, a huge, angular expanse of wall, intrudes rather clumsily into the spatial structure. The characteristic combination of glass, slabs of white stone and expanses of plaster is not here simply as Meier's architectural trademark; being in such great spatial proximity to Le Corbusier's buildings, the features of the formal language Meier derived from him acquire a reminiscent wilfulness eager to prove itself, probably for the first time, within the master's orbit. It should not, however, be assumed that this was what may have perplexed Meier so much about his design; for it seems that the architect was unable properly to reconcile his spatial structure, which, though not always practical and functional, is largely successful in terms of visual composition, with the restrictive shape of his site, and that he compensated for his frustration at the lack of scope for spatial development with a plethora of individual motifs that overlap, clash, and compete.

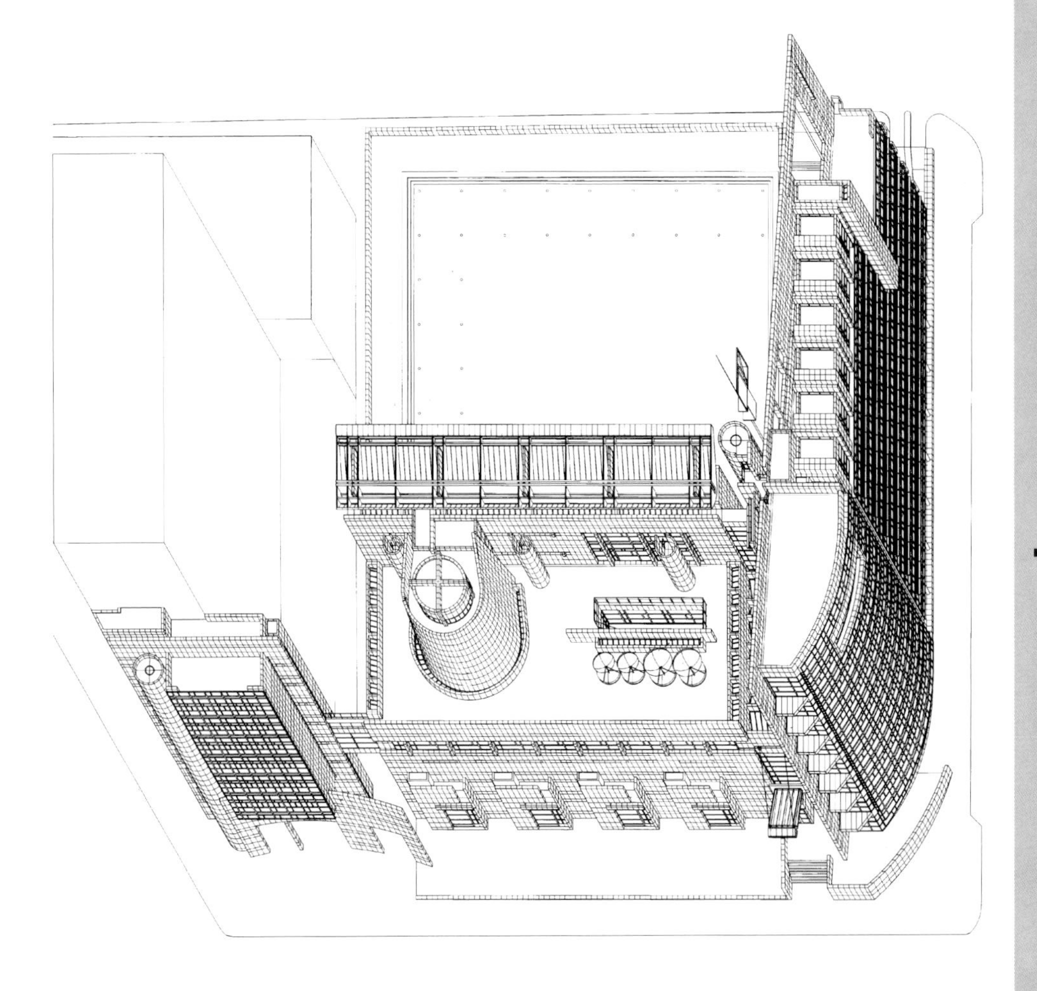

Constructed right up against the neighbouring buildings towards the Seine and the Parc Citroën, a subterranean telephone exchange reduces the site to an "L"-shape. Meier designed a complex of four buildings into this area, comprising offices on the river side and a production area towards the street.

Thus the ingenious window arrangements of the elegantly curved, glazed corner section are swamped by a mass of detail on which the opaque squares inset in each window segment impose an enervating staccato. That which, from within, charmingly dissects one's view of Paris into fragmentary, individually framed vedute looks from outside like a formalistic arithmetical problem. The huge, square aperture in which the projecting wall surface terminates acquires as few perspectives from the spatial disposition as the corner collision between flying roof and cylindrical stairway, which intersect in an unfortunate manner. The vague insights into the internal structure afforded by the flying roof create an effect that is solid and heavy rather than light, hermetically dense rather than transparent. The close juxtaposition of projecting and receding, overhanging and recessed elements and the contrast between intricately patterned structures and big, bloated ones causes the compact structural volume to disintegrate into innumerable, often extremely abrupt ideas. Mundane details such as windows inserted like building bricks look contrived where a smooth façade would have sufficed on its own and disruptive where existing formal elements are already competing for attention.
A.G.

The dynamic curve in the north-west corner of the office wing is open towards the Seine. The refined subdivision of the windows with their finely structured glazing is, however, lost amidst the small fussy details of the bars between panes.

Elevation, cross-section, site plan.
Framed by the long building tract to the west and north, a large section of the site has been turned into a garden.

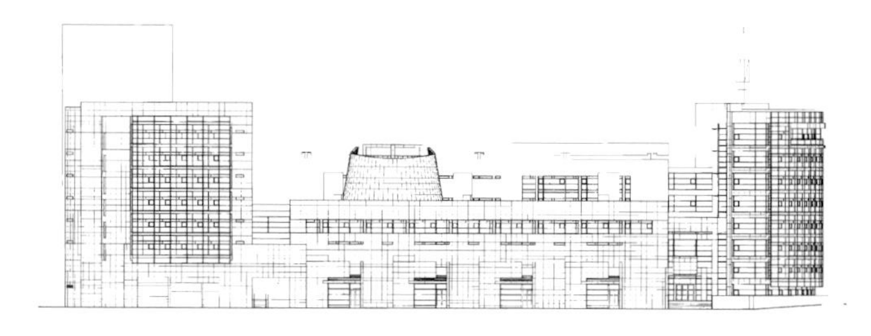

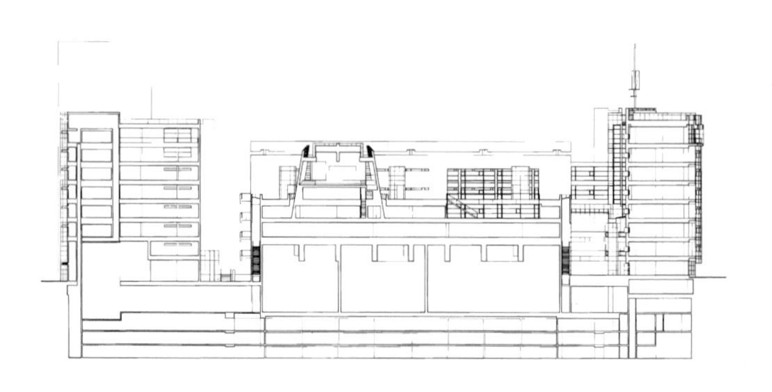

The multi-storey entrance foyer, flooded by natural light, forms the link between the office and studio tracts. Balconies, bridges and columns around the reception area which extend the full height of the room, all evoke a public square in a city. The continuous comings and goings in this area take place under the watchful eye of the security forces and remain an event exclusively reserved for the staff.

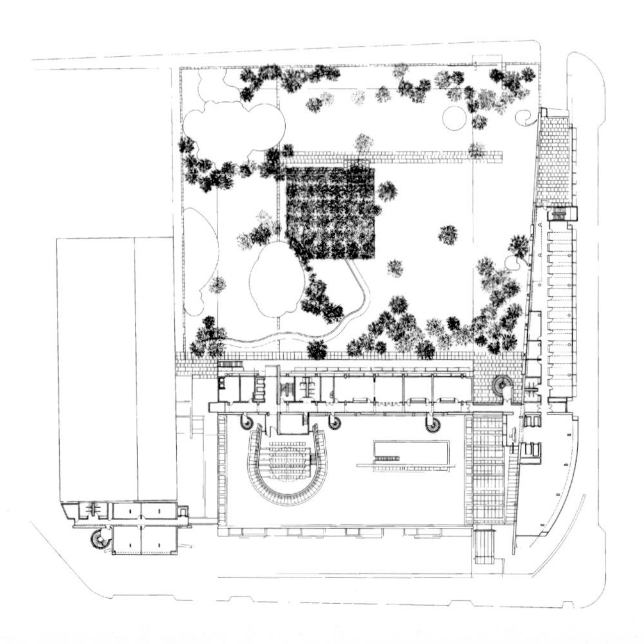

Headquarters of the Taxi-Drivers' Guild

Francis Soler

Completion 1989

This office building in the 19th Arrondissement stands at the acute-angled intersection of Rue de Meaux and Rue Armand-Carrel, of which the latter, pursuant to Haussmann's intentions, was driven through the quarter at the end of the 19th century. Haussmann's plan was realized only in part, however, because the requisite funding was unavailable and local opposition too strong. The extension that intersects with the broad Avenue Jean-Jaurès was not pushed through until a later date. Today the street represents an urbanists' intervention beneficial to through traffic but detrimental to the residential district. The young Parisian architect Francis Soler based his design on this conflict of interests.

One is immediately struck by his building's two very different façades: in the north-west, on the Rue de Meaux side, a smooth, elegantly conceived and carefully executed steel-and-glass skin with steel stairs behind it; in Rue Armand-Carrel, by contrast, a lively façade with projections and recesses, horizontal strip windows, and sharply tapering brise-soleils. Soler means these very dissimilar façades to point up the 'accident historique' occasioned by the irruption of Rue Armand-Carrel. He himself has stated that the south façade, in particular, is intended to lend clear expression to this 'breach'. It looks as if it had been broken off and subsequently reaffixed to the raw edge. Not so in Rue de Meaux, where the façade is aligned with the other buildings in the street and does not project or recede. This concept endows the building, which is situated in an exposed position but technically designed for straightforward office use, with a very special architectonic quality tailored to its site. In Soler's view, a building's relationship to its site is a factor crucial to its design and constitutes the sole justification for adopting unusual ideas.

The main entrance, slightly set back between the two façades, is on the corner. Situated one behind the other on the glass façade side are the two straight stairways required to cope with the considerable number of people entering and leaving the building. On a triangular ground-plan beyond the entrance are the office premises, which can be divided up into separate rooms as required and without effecting the load-bearing structure. Five hundred square metres are available on each of seven levels. The service area runs along the fire wall in the east, where additional light is supplied by a narrow courtyard.

A year before he completed this office building for the Taxi-Drivers' Guild, Soler's design for an international conference centre near the Eiffel Tower was enthusiastically hailed as a new 'Grand Projet de l'Etat'. It provided for three large glass boxes containing various conference rooms, a press centre, and a spacious hothouse. Although worked out in every detail, the project was killed off by its great expense and the opposition of influential local residents.

In 1995 Soler won 7th Prize in the competition to design the new office building for the German Federal Chancellor in Berlin. His scheme envisaged another glass solitaire which he described as a garden sculpture and a 'manifesto of modern politics'.

S.R.

Headquarters of the Taxi-Drivers' Guild

Despite the protests of the local residents, the Rue Armand-Carrel was driven through this quarter at the end of the 19th century. Francis Soler integrated this historical aspect in his architecture. The building's south façade with its projections and recesses is a reminder of the painful incision made in a formerly intact urban landscape.

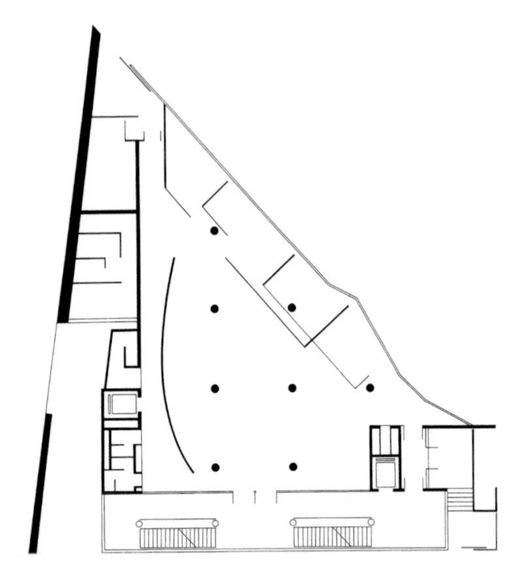

Floor plans of the ground floor office area with its flexible divisions. The stairways are behind the glass façade.

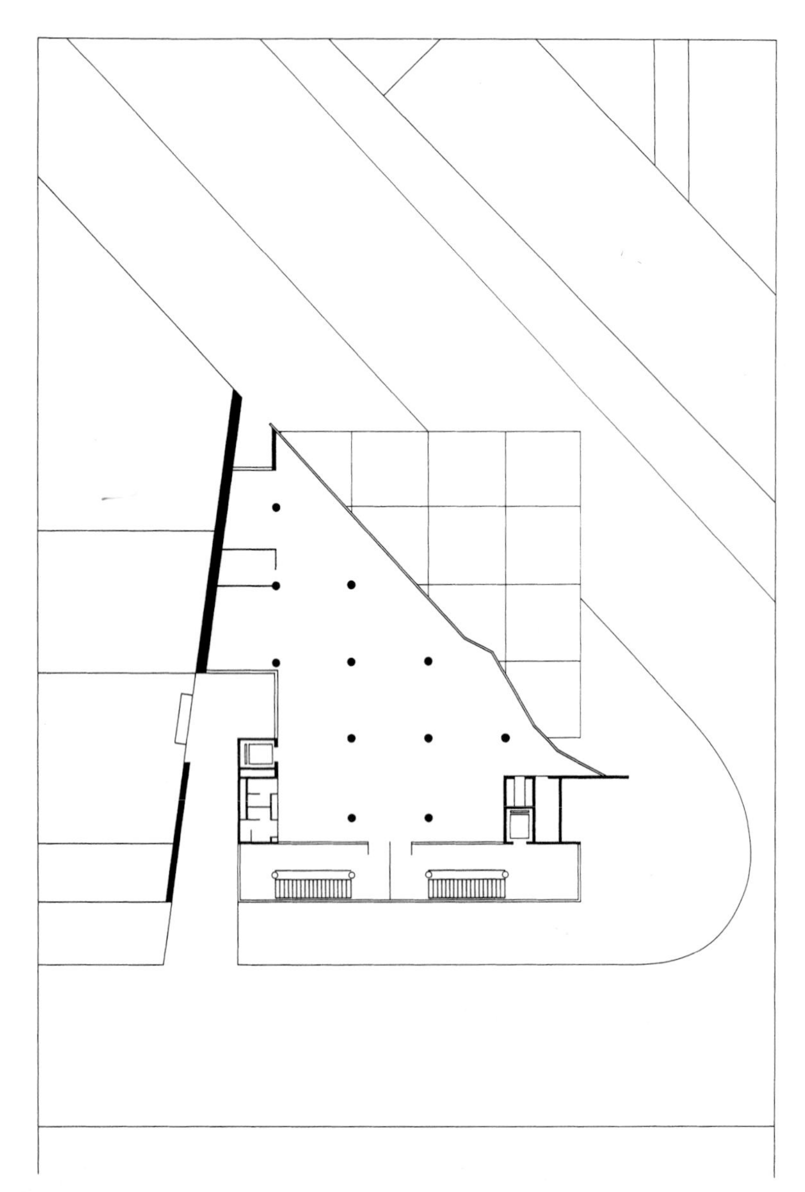

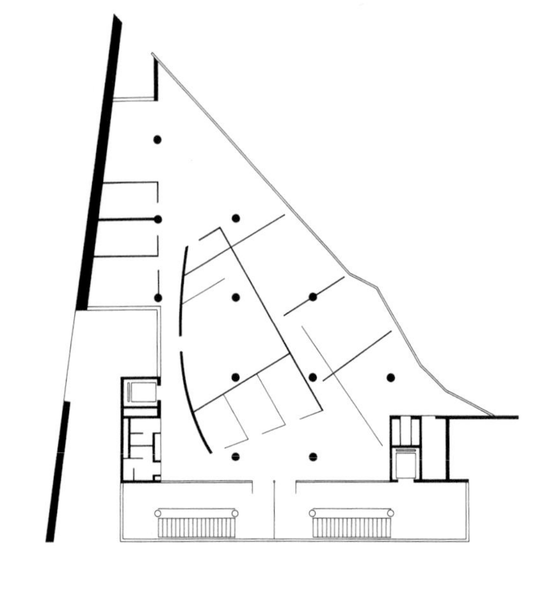

Details of the generously proportioned stairways and a view of the long, slightly curved landings.

American Center

Frank O. Gehry

Constructed 1991–94

Frank O. Gehry has so far completed three buildings on European soil, but others are being planned. Two of the projects he has completed since 1989 came into being far from architecture's metropolises and caused an uproar in the provinces: one at Weil am Rhein, in the south west of Germany where his dynamic museum sculpture for Vitra has become an architectural tourist attraction like Zaha Hadid's fire station and Tadao Ando's meditative seminary chapel; the other at Bad Oeynhausen, the inconspicuous Westphalian health resort just recently wrested from its architectural slumbers by Gehry's 'Energy Center'. Both are concentrated architectonic landscapes, abstract and complex, plastic and formally profuse.

In Paris, on the other hand, the site was of a different nature. Beset by the historical richness of the ancient metropolis on the Seine and assailed by its monuments to the future, it lies in Bercy, in the 12th Arrondissement, one of the main redevelopment areas on the right bank of the Seine, in the urbanistically maltreated east of the city. Bercy used to be Paris's 'wine depot', but almost nothing of that remains. Overlooked by the monstrous new Ministry of Finance, the narrow strip of land between the tracks of the Gare de Lyon, the Boulevard Périphérique and the Seine, now flanked by an expressway, has been subjected to radical rearrangement and reconstruction.

The site at Gehry's disposal formed the end of an elongated block containing a high-class selection of new dwellings situated between Rue de Pommard and the artificial greenery of the new Parc de Bercy. The plot had been deprived of its south-west corner, which was lopped off at an angle of 45° for reasons of town planning, so its ground-plan and surroundings, which owe so much to the 'new' Paris, challenged Gehry to make some unexpected gestures. Already acclaimed as a virtuoso in the sculptural composition of architectural forms, he based his design on an idea that is clearly suggestive of classical façade sequences and exploits the antithesis between the building line and the park in a series of contrastive collisions and puzzling, associative superimpositions. On the street side, where it is entirely faced with limestone slabs, the American Center creates a rather austere and withdrawn impression, displaying a thoroughly dignified restraint that purports to know what it owes to the honourable tradition of the Parisian corridor street. Gehry readily adheres to Rue de Pommard's new building line and translates it into a perpendicular wall whose smooth expanse is subordinated to a disciplined window geometry. The deeply recessed window jambs suggest a stone building of considerable bulk, whereas the rational rhythm of the façade is that of a somewhat austere office building. Slightly surprising, however, are the double overhangs that cause the wall of the first two upper stories to project in a peculiar manner, creating a precarious contrast to the recessed ground-floor zone beneath it and faintly reminding one from a distance of the abstract, rational, formal geometries of the Revolutionary architects.

Gehry continues this austere, seemingly context-conscious façade into the square for another few metres, thereby creating a clearly defined edge, a firmly delineated corner. Only then, after this distinct break, do the rhythm and dramaturgy change, setting the building in motion. Gehry has made effective use of the lopped south-west corner of his site. This is where the American Center's main entrance is situated, in the façade sequence giving straight on the square. It is there, facing away from the street and framed by the other ranges of buildings, that the architecture explodes, bursting the bonds of precision, and that the architect allows the formal language he has perfected in recent years to develop its full, sculptural autonomy. The smooth walls break open. Distorted individual shapes flow forth and recede, shatter the building's stereometric cohesion, and dissolve its outlines into a topography of dramatic contrasts, inclined planes, abrupt protrusions, varying heights, and deep incisions. It is only here, facing away from the street, that Gehry takes all those architectonic liberties whose spatial and formal inventions are founded, first and foremost, on their inherent autonomy. The lobby that corresponds to the square, its walls faced with the same stone as the exterior, lies beyond the glassed-in entrance. The boundaries between inside and outside are meant to be fluid. Within, facing the square's open expanse, the spatial structure becomes condensed into an abstract distillation of urban elements. Street, square, and the recently popular typology of the Parisian inner courtyard provide the keynotes of a spatial mise-en-scène sustained by the complexity of its spa-

Seen from the street, Gehry's building appears austere and withdrawn. Faced with sand-coloured limestone slabs, the American Center has an appropriately reserved air, complying with the architecture of existing structures in the Rue Pommard. The smooth expanse of the perpendicular wall is subordinated to a disciplined window geometry. The deeply recessed window jambs suggest a stone building of considerable bulk, whereas the rational rhythm of the façade is that of an austere office building.

tial penetrations, visual angles, and luminous dramaturgy. Primarily accessible from this central lobby are the series of public rooms: a theatre, an often deserted restaurant, and a travel agency that shares the same fate. A number of stairways provide regulars and visitors with access to the upper floors, whose rooms follow the pattern that is doubtless proper to an intercontintental cultural institute, although it was neglected to supplement the exhibition rooms, language laboratories, studios, apartments and inevitable offices with one very important facility: a library. Rather small in relation to its surroundings, the building contains 18,400 square metres of floor space. Over and above its function and architectural aspirations, it was intended to perform a symbolic task: to exemplify, through the medium of a striking and original 'exchange architecture', the intercultural dialogue which, in the case of 'the American in Paris', is fraught with a myth all its own. As a Californian in Paris, Gehry has expressed that dialogue in an abstract collage that distils its elements from the city's architectural memory and, by sculpturally remoulding them, confronts us with the spatial inventions of his architectural imagination.
A.G.

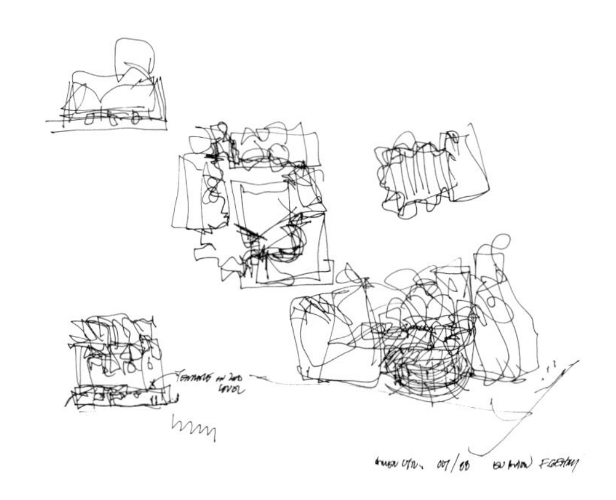

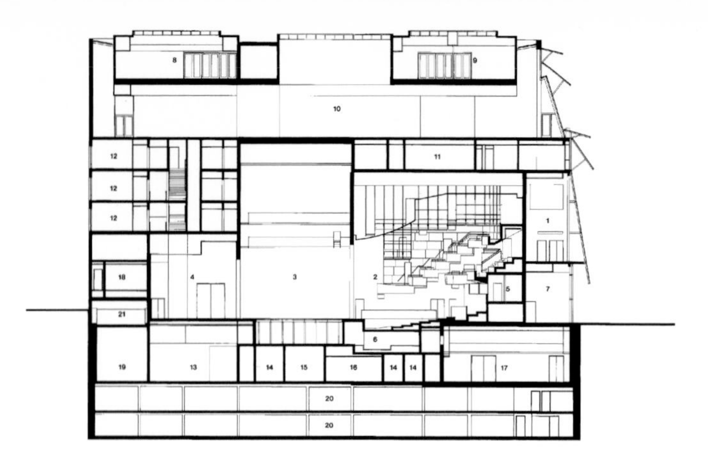

Sketches showing cross-sections, floor and site plans.
The central area is occupied by the foyer, from which access is gained principally to the rooms frequented by the public, some of which can also be leased to third parties, such as a travel agency. Visitors can gain easy access to the different levels via a multiplicity of staircases. These lead to exhibition rooms, language laboratories, studios, apartments and administrative offices. One important facility was however overseen: a library.

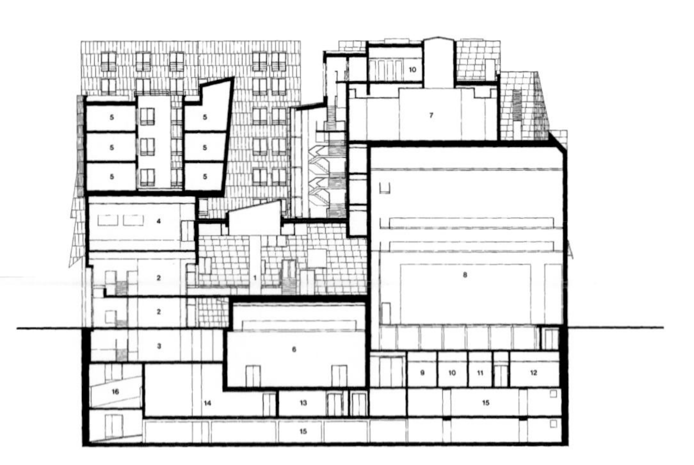

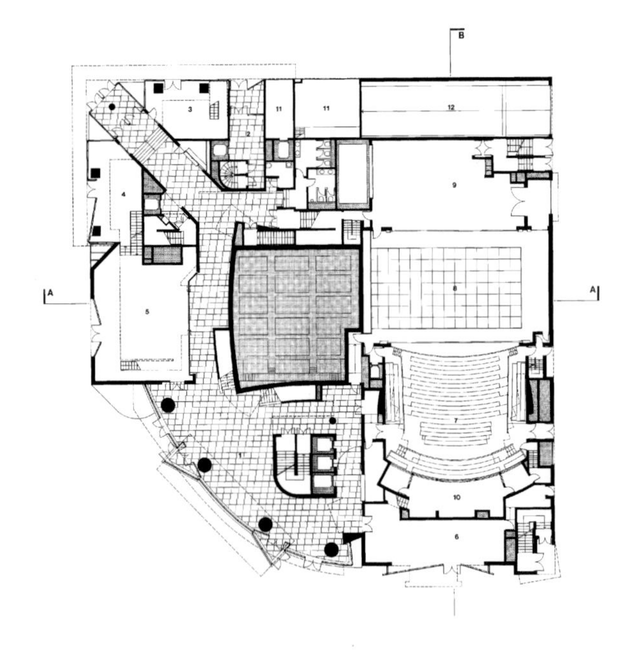

Opposite the open space which leads into the Parc Bercy, between the American Center, the Seine and the Palais Omnisport, the architecture becomes dynamic. This is where the main entrance is located and this is where rhythm and dramaturgy change. New sculptural possibilities are opened up.

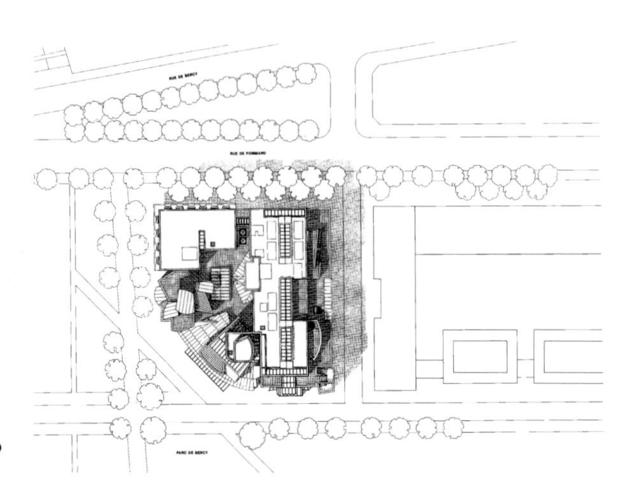

The sombre façade fronting the road is continued a few metres into the open space, before the smooth walls break open, distorted shapes shatter the building's stereometric cohesion, and dissolve its outlines into a topography of dramatic contrasts, inclined planes, abrupt protrusions, varying heights, and deep incisions.

View of the lobbies and the auditorium. The boundaries between the interior and exterior spaces are meant to be fluid. Within, facing the square's open expanse, the spatial structure becomes condensed into an abstract distillation of urban elements. Street, square, and the recently popular typology of the Parisian courtyard provide the keynotes of a spatial mise-en-scène sustained by the complexity of its spatial penetrations, visual angles, and luminous dramaturgy.

Apartment House and Post Office in Rue Oberkampf

Frédéric Borel

Completion 1993

Those who walk the streets of Paris must sometimes climb in order to reach an inferior destination – as in the case of Rue Oberkampf, which steadily ascends a gentle incline as it runs eastward. For this thoroughfare in the 11th Arrondissement is just a plain street, not a grand boulevard, still less a majestic avenue. Well off the tourist track, it takes any visitor who has strayed into this noisy quarter into the midst of the disintegration afflicting a capital city in the throes of great social distortions. The stone residue of a former cinema has been converted into a gleaming, chromium-plated yuppy bar, whereas plaster is flaking off the dismal dwellings across the street. Filled with shops, exotic restaurants and small workshops, and pierced by courtyards that delve deep into its block structure, this is nevertheless a lively neighbourhood in which both sides of life are readily visible. The two opposites are sometimes separated only by the width of a street, and they often resemble those of Rue Oberkampf.

The 'reality of the city' and, specifically, of this particular area with its complex social structure and history, has, according to Frédéric Borel, been discernible since November 1993 from and in No. 113, Rue Oberkampf. Under the auspices of Paris's post office building programme of the 1980s, the architect has taken up the challenge of designing a structure to fill a vacant lot almost 90 metres deep but only 20 metres wide. Borel has woven material, form and function into a remarkable complex of 80 apartments, a shop, and a ground-floor post office giving on the street. Since 1989, 'Opération Poste' has provided some 1500 post office personnel with rented accommodation that is not only cheap (it only costs some one-fifth of their salary) but cleverly designed. Moreover, the architecture that Paris has acquired through the post office's subsidized housing programme (which which has so far produced a total of 28 new buildings) is not just cheap, off-the-peg stuff; some of it is made to measure and of high quality.

Visible from afar in the washed-out, grey monotony of the street is a pale trident: the entrance façade, which, having afforded a generous view of the sunken inner courtyard, develops upward in a series of fissures and gradations. The building strikes a defiant note, as if wanting to show off its corners and edges. It does not, for all that, degenerate into an architectural exclamation mark. Why not? Because the street itself is reflected in its structural multiformity; because this small and far from ideal world is mirrored in the 'microcosm' of its architectural language and deliberately interpreted by means of the tension and eloquence of its architectural vocabulary; and, above all, because the building's gesture of invitation – the view of the courtyard from the street - employs modern methods to re-evoke the post office's formerly integrative function as a 'meeting-place'. One's gaze falls on the sometimes bizarre and formally very elaborate cubes that jut into the foreground; on the simple, externally identifiable studio apartments or the variously conceived living accommodation for young couples; on projections and protrusions; on flush windows or the façade layers generously peeled off the wall surfaces and their glass interstices; and on a footbridge that boldly slices across the air space above the courtyard, which has been carefully designed as a residents' garden.

This expressive building's axonometric plan recalls a fragmented Cubist landscape: its daring disarticulation gives rise to constant collisions between substance and space, and it displays an incessant alternation of introversion and architectural exhibitionism, of the private and the public. Strangely enough, however, despite its architectural stridency and because it respects its structural ambience (the eaves and their downward development from the street and the volumes and their relative disposition), it fits into Rue Oberkampf in a remarkably unostentatious manner.
G.M.

Apartment House and Post Office in Rue Oberkampf

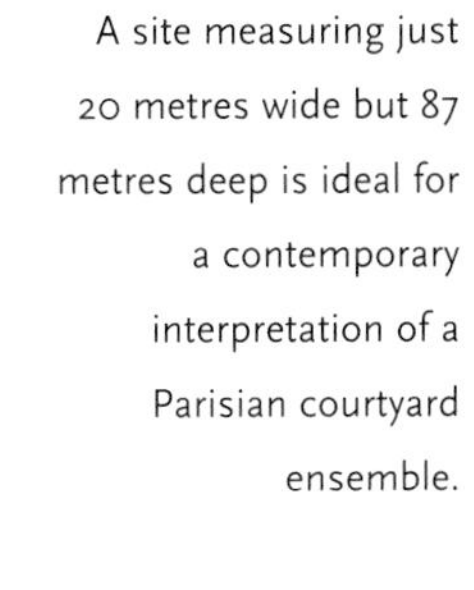

A site measuring just 20 metres wide but 87 metres deep is ideal for a contemporary interpretation of a Parisian courtyard ensemble.

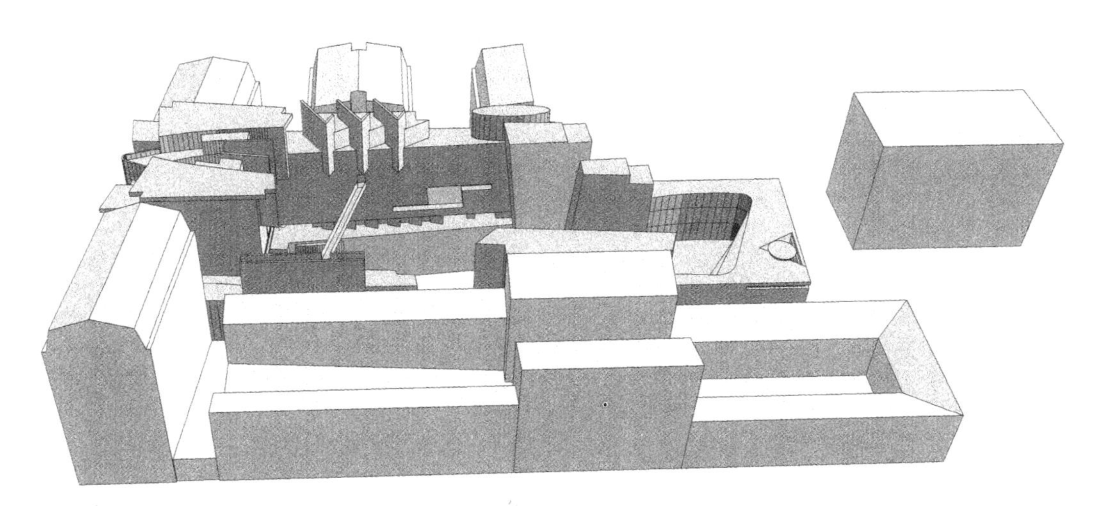

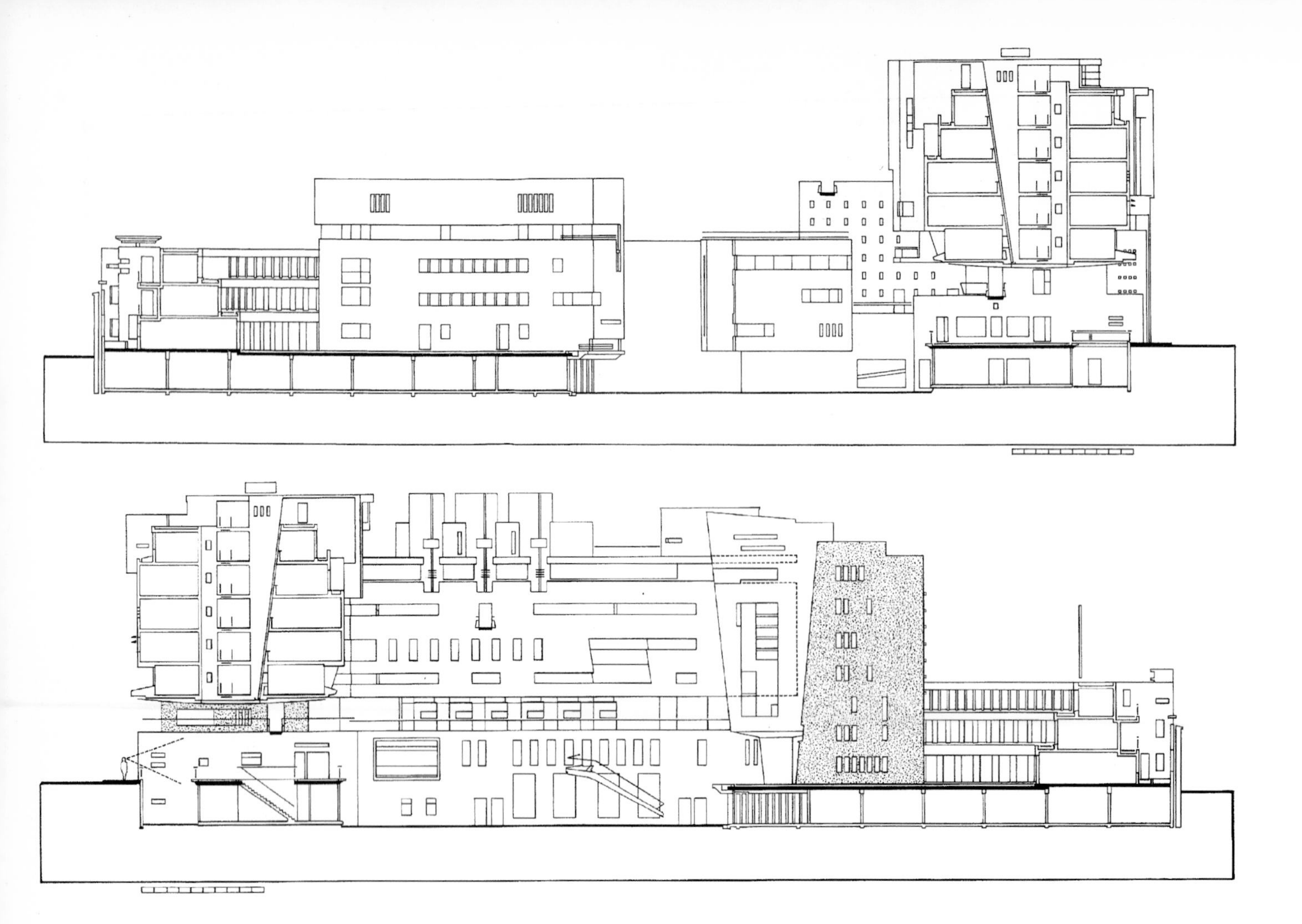

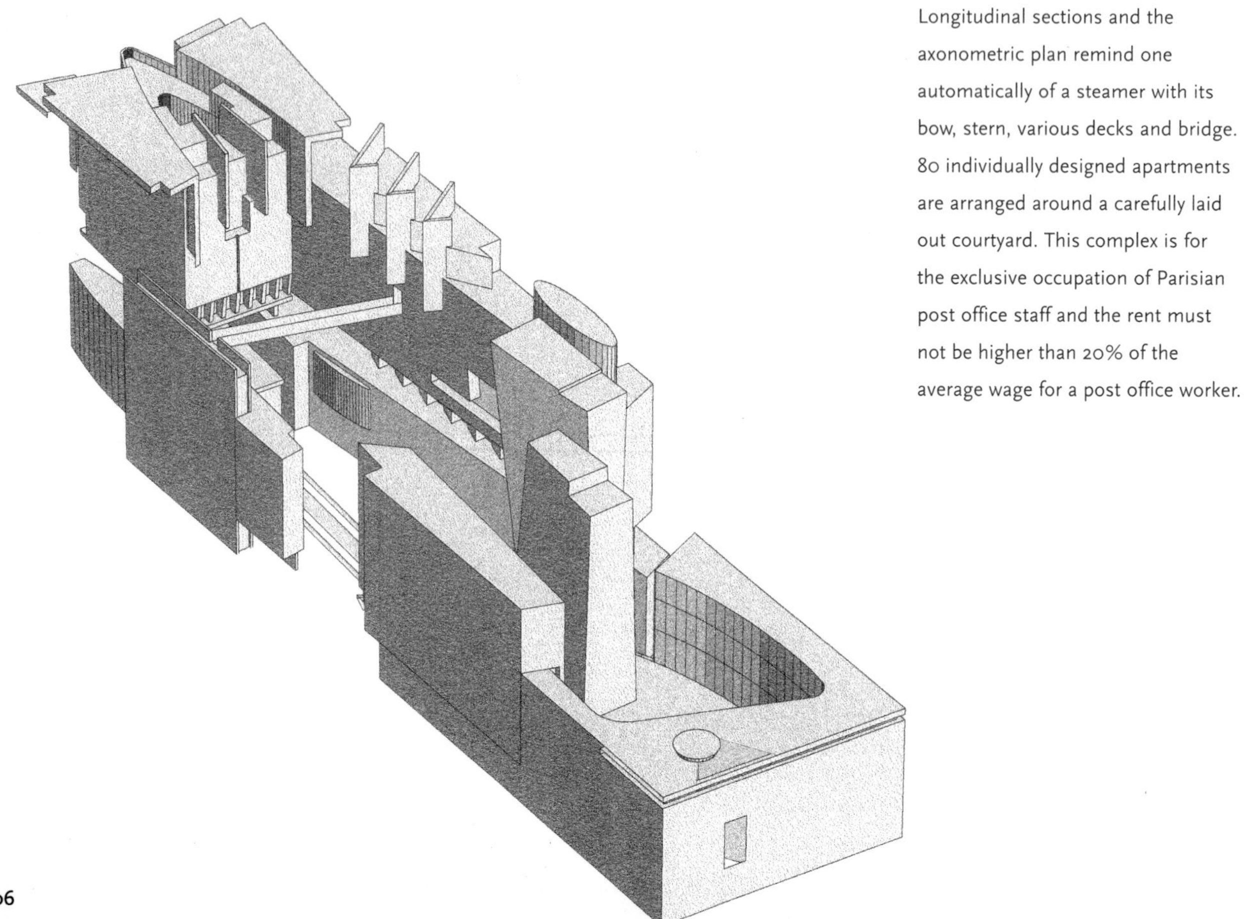

Longitudinal sections and the axonometric plan remind one automatically of a steamer with its bow, stern, various decks and bridge. 80 individually designed apartments are arranged around a carefully laid out courtyard. This complex is for the exclusive occupation of Parisian post office staff and the rent must not be higher than 20% of the average wage for a post office worker.

The courtyard is designed as a geometric variant on the garden layout typical of such quarters. The open space is dramatically sliced in two by a narrow footbridge. Curious passers-by can gain an impression of the whole complex from the street.

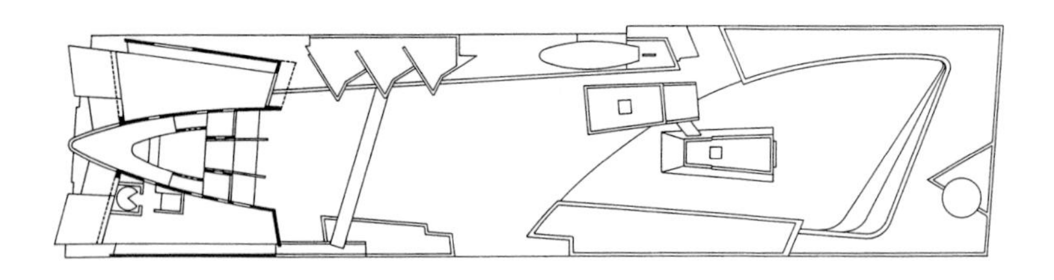

Favouring an expressive feeling of space with projections, towers, and twisted cubes, the architect ignored rational constraints in many elements of his plan. On the street side, the building, with its series of fissures and gradations, towers seven storeys high.

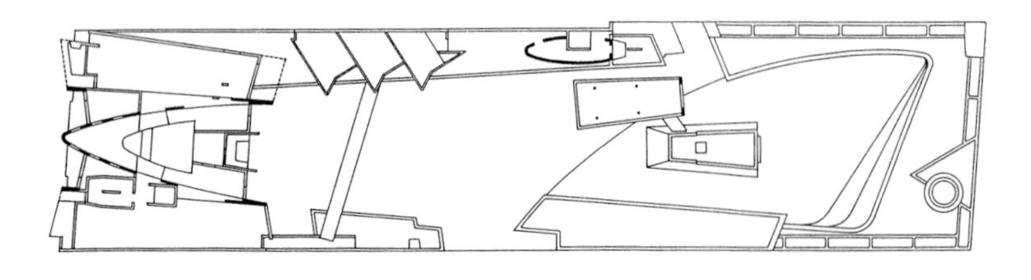

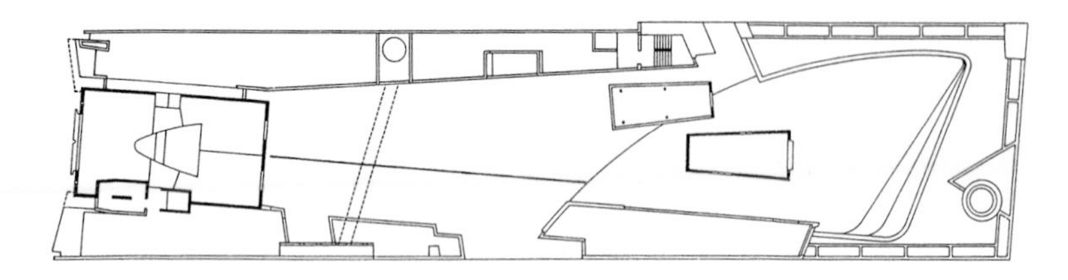

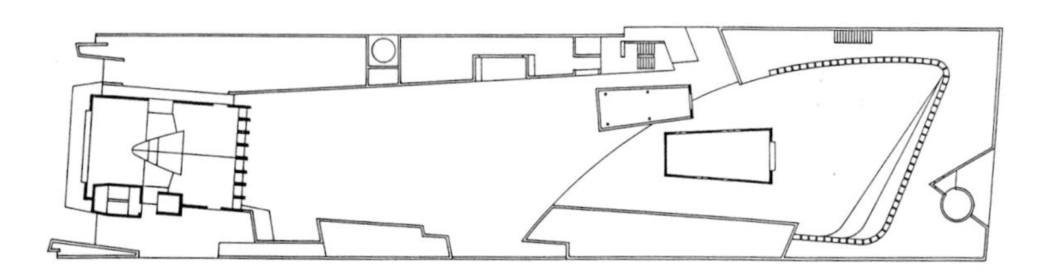

Like stalagmites in a cave, three individually designed housing segments rise out of the back third of the courtyard, each constructed of entirely different materials and with a different rhythm to the façade. Coming down the steps is like leaving an architectural space rocket and stepping back onto the earth.

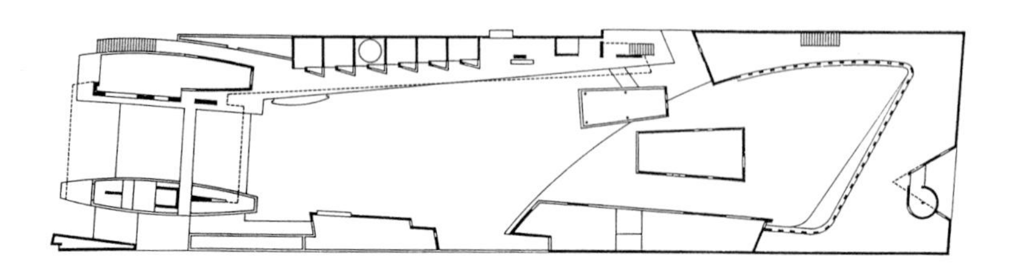

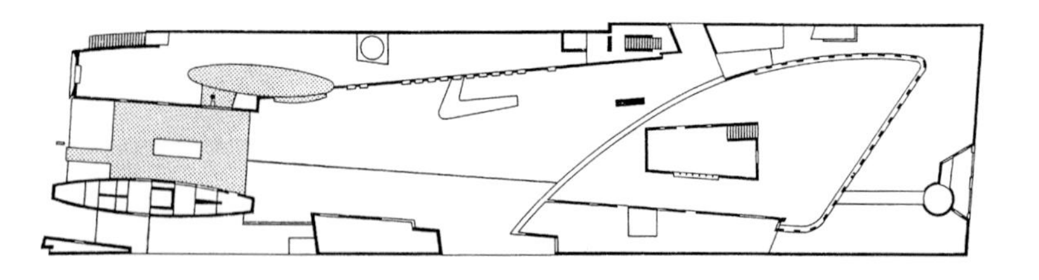

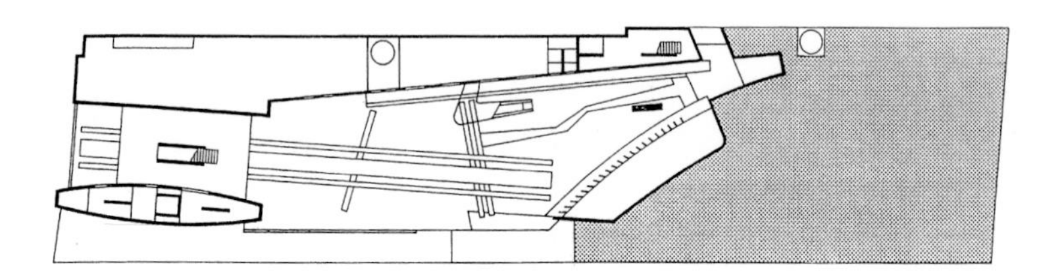

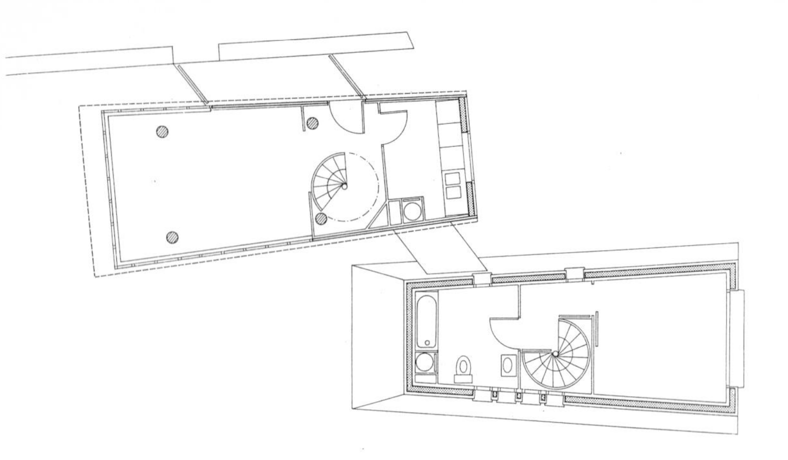

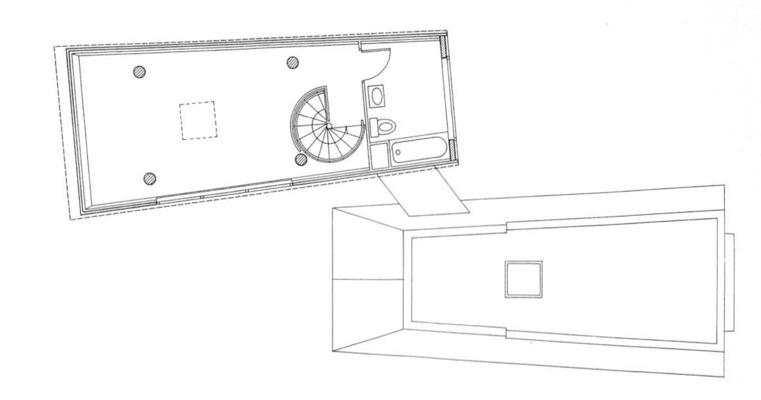

Rue Oberkampf in the 11th Arrondissement is a plain but lively street. Number 113 draws attention to itself with its bright entrance front divided up by different gradations.

Light streams in through the various openings in the individually designed living accommodation. At the counter in the post office, however, all staff work under the same conditions.

1
Toutes opérations
2
Toutes opérations
3

The Bibliothèque Jussieu Project

Rem Koolhaas

Project 1992

'We are setting urbanism against architecture. Architecture excludes possibilities by its definition of space; urbanism, on the other hand, generates potentials.' The Dutch architect Rem Koolhaas likes to dramatize urban space, as witness Euralille, his already completed large-scale project.

In 1989 Koolhaas entered the Bibliothèque Nationale François Mitterrand competition (see p. 42) and received an honourable mention. Four years later he was commissioned to design a far smaller library for the Université Pierre et Marie Curie, known as Université Jussieu, situated only a few hundred metres away, north of the Jardin des Plantes. This design bears a rudimentary resemblance to the one he produced for the Bibliothèque Nationale François Mitterrand.

The university's existing buildings dating from the 1960s are characterized by strict rationality. The multi-storey blocks with their steel-and-glass façades are of latticework construction and in stark contrast to the turn-of-the-century buildings surrounding them. The campus is dominated by a single high-rise block containing the administrative offices. The new, uniform buildings were left unfinished in 1968. After the Paris riots in May of that year, when the campus became a major focus of student unrest, the authorities 'punished' the university by discontinuing work. Incomplete sections were simply walled up.

Koolhaas integrates his library building in this rational and anonymous area in the midst of the city, with its disused vacuum of a campus, by means of a design that is externally just as rational. Inside, however, the unremarkable building displays an engaging complexity. Visitors gain access to the upper storeys via an ingenious system of connecting passages, not a central lobby and staircase. The rooms and levels, most of them open, are dissected into various shapes by flat ramps described as bands, so 35 % of the storeys' floor space is not horizontal. The result, housed in a complex three-dimensional structure, is a multiplicity of ground-plans that facilitate the widest possible variety of functions and present the visitor with many different visual experiences.

On closer inspection, the building proves to consist of two libraries situated one above the other: the science library, with its relatively large proportion of closed stock-rooms, some of which are inset in the floor; and, above it, the humanities library, with its open stock-rooms. The two libraries are separated by the entrance hall and reception area, from which the Métro station is directly accessible.

Koolhaas regards the building less as a building than as a public space. It is a kind of skeleton for the compression and stratification of urban space, whose better utilization is the design's foremost aim. The entire building is encased in a transparent skin of non-reflecting glass made up of huge, irregular sheets that overlap like shingles. Brightly illuminated at night and visible from a long way off, the library is intended to become the new centre of the university and the 5th Arrondissement.

Government coffers being empty, the chances of putting this scheme into effect are, unfortunately, nil.
S.R.

The Bibliothèque Jussieu Project

The Jussieu University south of the Ile de St.-Louis consists of multi-storey blocks with steel-and-glass façades of latticework construction. Within this rational area Koolhaas integrated a glass library with a unique interior organisation.

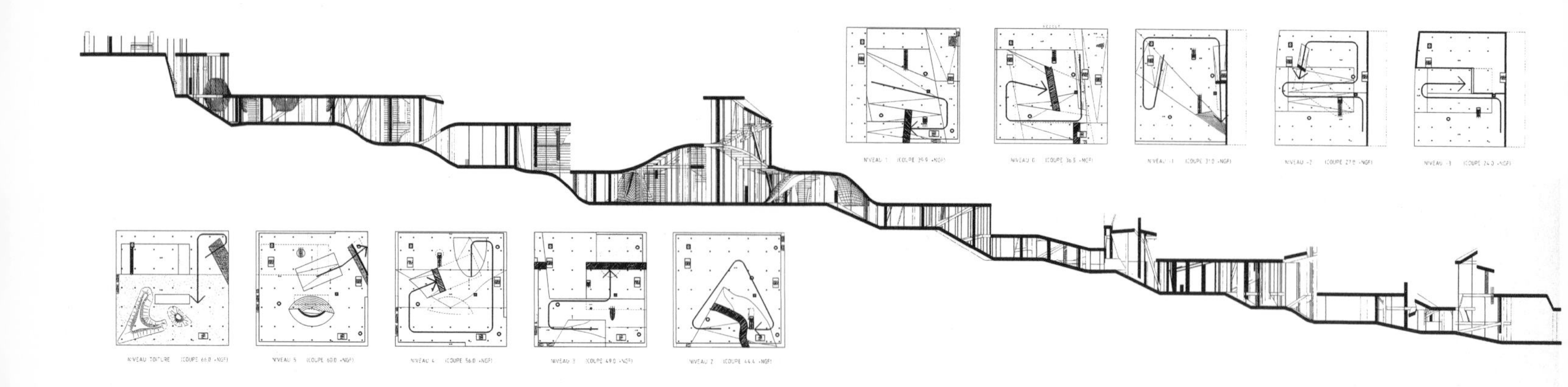

Floor plans, cross-sections and photo of the model of the building, which is defined by its flat ramp "bands".

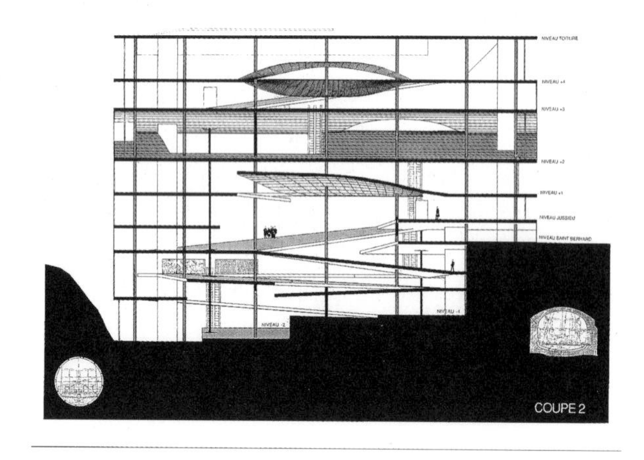

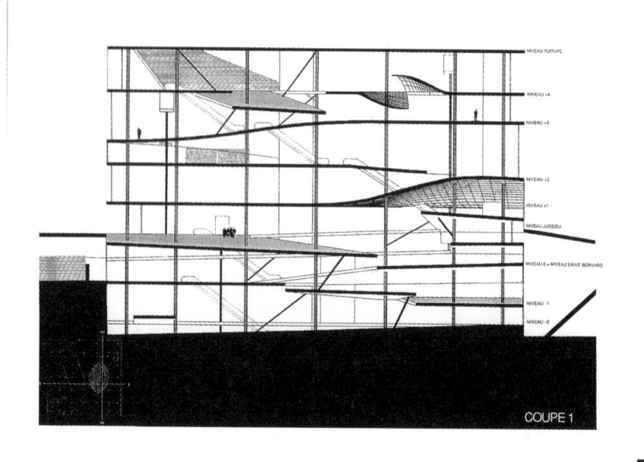

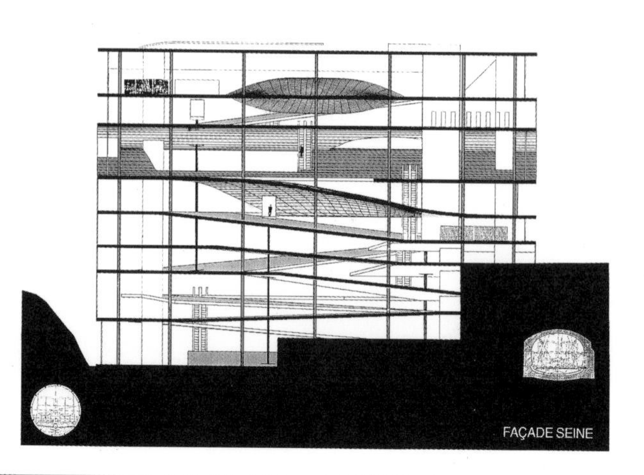

André Citroën Park

Patrick Berger, Gilles Clement, Jean Paul Viguier,
Jean François Jodry, Alain Provost

Completion 1992–3

Despite its density, Paris has always been a city not only of stone but of squares and parks whose conformation has endowed its layout with some memorable shapes and places. The most recent parks have augmented and enriched this scenario forming a remarkable trio: La Villette, the prototypal example in the north of the city, Parc de Bercy in the east, and Parc Citroën in the west. Common to all three is a conceptual aspiration that differentiates them from traditional green spaces and recalls the typological and iconographic programme underlying the gardens and parks of the 17th and 18th centuries. Parc Citroën exemplifies this in an exceptionally ambitious manner, and does so in surroundings that would lead one to expect anything but a place for contemplation and reflection on the arcana of garden design.

This park, too, which came into being not far from the Seine on the site of the former Citroën works, is the centrepiece of a ZAC (Zone d'Aménagement concerté) project. A substantial 13 hectares in extent, it is surrounded by a mundane medley of housing estates, office complexes, railway lines, and roads. Its boundaries seem to lose themselves in the rather fortuitous and amorphous outlines of this disparate setting, which derives as little cohesion from Richard Meier's architecture in the north (see p. 88) as it does from the mediocre housing development in Rue Balard or Michel Kagan's elongated apartment and studio building on its southern periphery. It seemed logical, therefore, that this unexpected vacuum, whose original function offered no points of reference, should be remodelled in an entirely novel and self-assured manner. This is far from immediately apparent to the casual eye, however. Only detailed examination discloses the consistent nature of a design that reveals itself to be a basic shape in which elaborate complexity and geometrical rationality complement each other.

The whole layout is subject to an abstract logic that relates and unites its varied manifestations in the form of a natural and artificial, botanical and architectural event.

Seen from the Seine, the park's components are grouped around a central stretch of grass in accordance with a ground-plan whose shape leads the eye from west to east. Although the plot's iregular boundaries break up its underlying symmetries, they do not disrupt its inherent dialogue. A pathway that cuts diagonally across the park inscribes a line that runs sharply counter to its spatial flow. Not included in the competition design, this transverse connection derives simply from the rather banal fact that the park's design was entrusted to two different teams whose submissions displayed surprising affinities.

The north side of the park was entrusted to Gilles Clement and Patrick Berger, landscape architect and architect respectively, and the south to Team Provost and Viguier/Jodrey. Both areas present a series of thematic designs of which each is important in itself but all engage in a dialogue via the central expanses of grass and water. The pale limestone square of the 'Jardin Blanc', filled with deciduous trees, provides a counterpoint to the far more massive granite architecture and evergreens of the 'Jardin Noir'. The 'Jardins Sériels', surmounted by glass greenhouses, are balanced by the cold, chiselled cubatures of the nymphaea. The 'Jardin en Mouvement', a never motionless bamboo grove, has its counterpart in the 'Jardin des Métamorphoses', a wild area intended to be left entirely to the mercy of nature's ecological whims. The sculptural architectures of the 'portico' have been allotted a rock garden. Interrelationships are of a formal, intrinsic and symbolic nature. Glass and stone, the seemingly natural and the artificially contrived, the geometrical and organic, the concealed and the wide-open, the botanical and architectural – all these are thematized in dialectical and superimposed relationships and give rise to morphological transformations.

Water is accorded a very important role in this skilful dialogue between vegetation and architecture on the banks of the Seine: as a strictly regulated canal that flanks the central expanse of grass; as the choreographer of the 80 fountains that transform the paved area in front of the orangerie buildings on the east side of the park into a lively aquatic display; as standing water and water in motion; as rivulet and spring.

Those who stroll through the park with its geometrical layout in mind and a printed guide in their pocket may soon discern its inherent attributes, formal relationships and symbolic meanings. Those denied such aids will still be able to take pleasure in its multifarious happenings.

A.G.

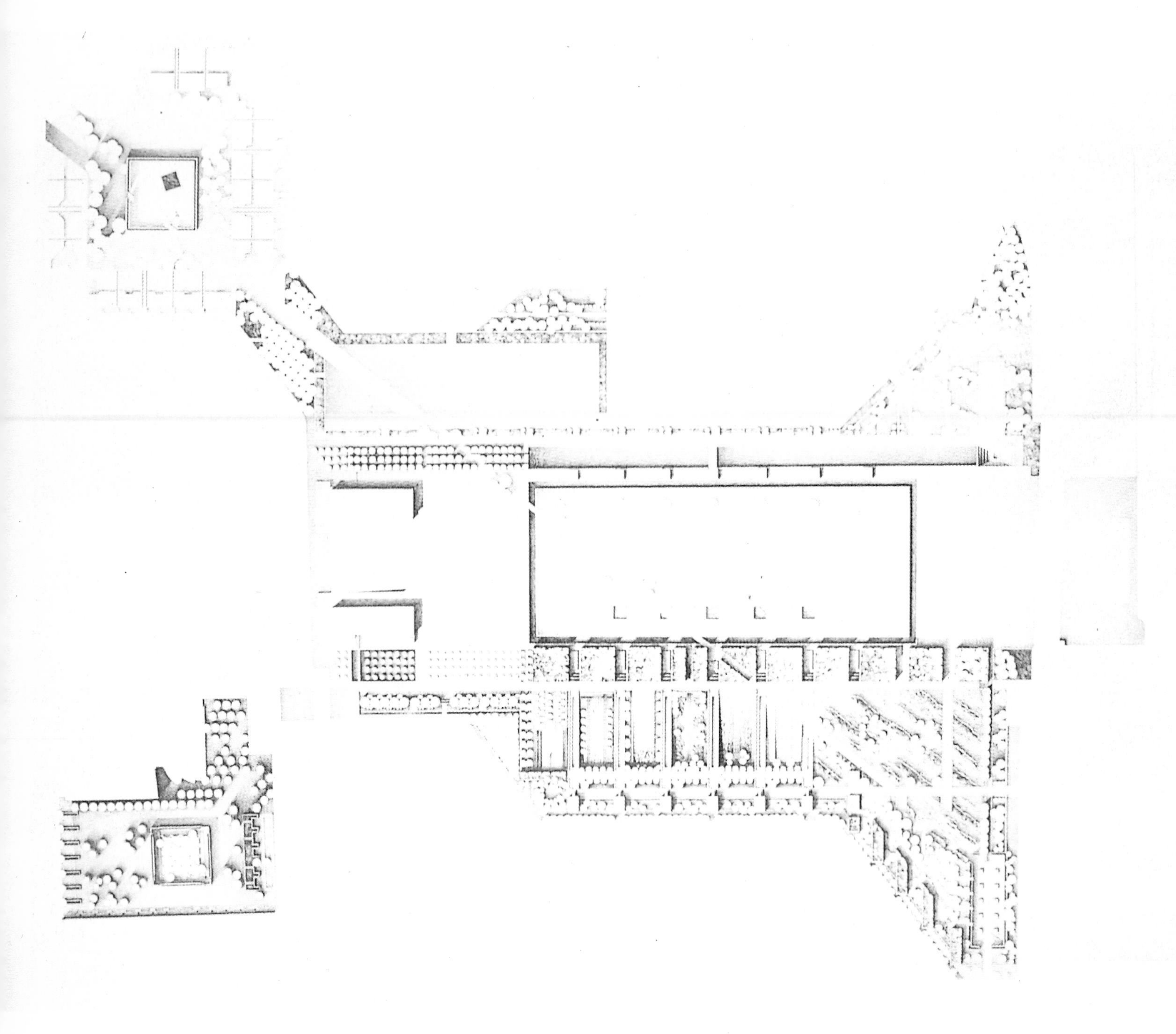

Site plan.

The park was designed by two teams. Gilles Clement and Patrick Berger were responsible for the northern sector and the Team Provost and Viguier/Jodry for the southern. The different sections of the park are arranged around a central stretch of grass. Although the plot's symmetry is disrupted by its irregular boundaries, an inherent dialogue is attained. A diagonal pathway that forms a central axis across the site, inscribes a line that runs sharply counter to its spatial flow. The thematic structure of the two sectors harmonize well, creating an overall design which is complementary in its geometrical rationality and complexity.

The park extends over an area of 13 hectares and is surrounded by a mundane medley of housing estates, office complexes, railway lines, and roads. These provide a stark contrast to the strong architectural and landscaping features.

Sketches for the central glass "orangerie" pavilion and the architec-tural elements in the "Jardins sérielles" (Clement/Berger).

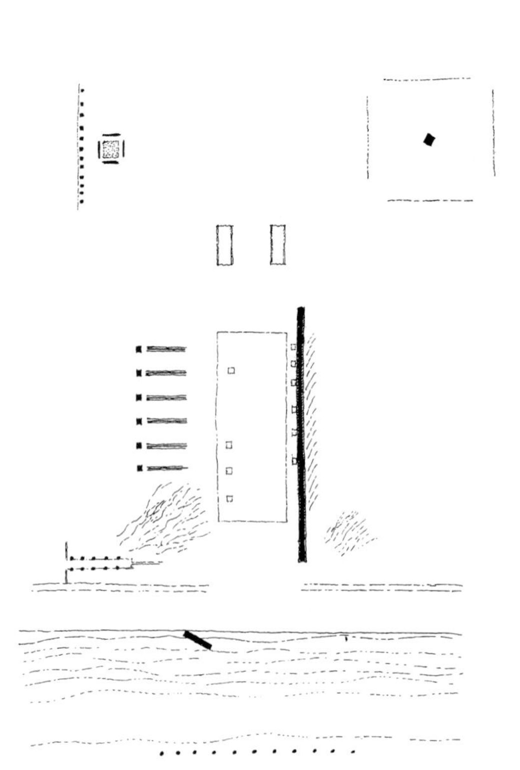

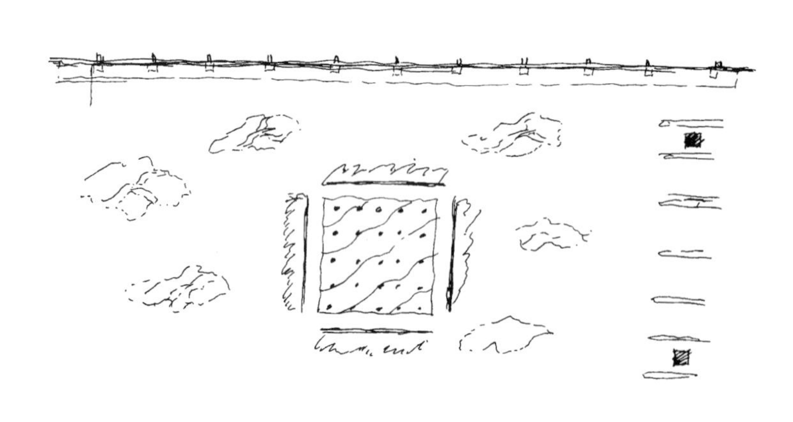

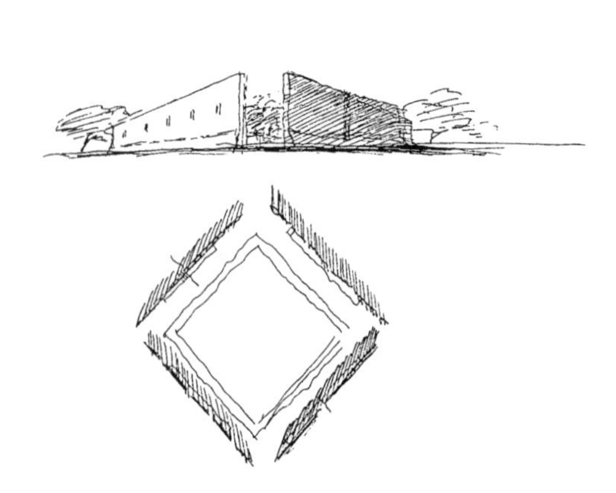

The complex as a whole is governed by an abstract logic. The varying elements, be they man-made or natural, architectural or natural, are interrelated and complementary. The light limestone wall (below) for example, around the "hortus conclusus" in the "Jardin Blanc" (Provost and Viguier/Jodry) provides only tantalizing glimpses of the vegetation within the enclosure.

The porticoed or pillared gateway (left) marks the western end of the park walk.

View across the large canal towards the south of the park showing the clearcut geometrical form of the nymphaea.

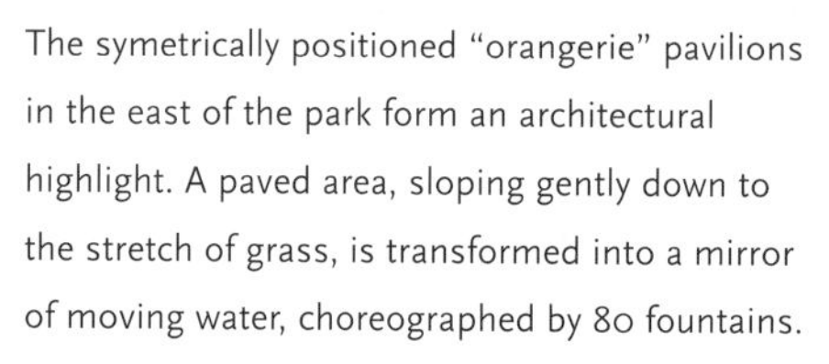

The symetrically positioned “orangerie” pavilions in the east of the park form an architectural highlight. A paved area, sloping gently down to the stretch of grass, is transformed into a mirror of moving water, choreographed by 80 fountains.

View of one of the “orangeries”; despite their fragile appearance, the transparent pavilions, carried on slender wooden supports, are impressive structures, standing out against the otherwise bland architecture of the quarter.

The Parc de Bercy

Bernard Huet, F.F.L. Architectes
(Marylène Ferrand, Jean-Pierre Feugas, Bernard Le Roy)

Landscape design: Ian Le Caisne, Philippe Raguin

Completion 1997

Completed after the Parc de la Villette in the north and the Parc André Citroën in the west of Paris, the Parc de Bercy in the east recently became the city's third such large-scale amenity.

Bercy was a focal point of APUR's planning from 1978 onwards. It was also one of the most difficult, because Bercy, a former wine trade centre whose picturesque but dilapidated architectural fabric had become as obsolete as it was steeped in history, was subjected to restructuring of a particularly drastic nature. The new Ministry of Finance was followed by the grassed-over, truncated pyramid of the Palais Omnisport, the American Center, which strove (and strives) to assert itself both architecturally and as an institution, and an adjacent housing development of rather solid and unspectacular design. In scale and arrangement, these new buildings have firmly eliminated the picturesque and down-at-heel complexity of the former wine quarter and replaced its tangled obscurity with the readily discernible clarity of an orthogonal layout based on Haussmann's plans.

The park is intended to provide this new architectural structure with a new focal point, a kind of core that can accommodate the urban dialectic's sensual and emotional energies.

The park is situated in a regular rectangle which, though running parallel to the Seine, is separated from it – like its companion-piece, the Parc André Citroën – by multi-lane roads. Its other margins are dominated by Frank Gehry's restrained architectural bizarreries and the bourgeois façades of the new buildings in Rue de Pominard. The towers of the new national library loom up, stern and statuesque, on the other side of the Seine. Although these repositories of universal knowledge are not alone in conveying nothing of the history of their site, which was anything but a seat of intellectual intercourse and became one of fascist barbarism's numerous trans-shipment centres during the 1940s, when the central depot for confiscated Jewish property was established at Tolbiac, the designers of the new park across the river were very much at pains to find some way of perpetuating the memory of the Bercy of old, which, though far more innocuous, was important in terms of urban history. They planned to create Jardins de la mémoire, or gardens of remembrance, in which a few relics of the former wine quarter could be preserved in a newly defined and designed, 'picturesque' context.

The basis of the design is a clear-cut geometrical structure that divides the park into three squares of equal size. Each of these squares is subdivided into nine smaller quadrangles, the resultant grid being defined by paths in the form of paved walks. On this rational, regular, rectangular layout the architects have superimposed a second, thematic layer that assigns each area a focal point and may, when viewed in sequence, be interpreted as a kind of archaeological clue to the genius loci on the one hand and the iconography of the park on the other. The first square was conceived as an expanse of grass intended to be played and disported on, and, at the same time, to awaken memories of meadows in the country. Next comes a second square containing so-called thematic beds whose rather artificial arrangements of flowers and plants demonstrate the regulation of nature and are also meant to recall the gardens of the small country houses that characterized Bercy's preliminary development in the 18th century, prior to its conversion into a wine depot. Only one of the original, barrel-vaulted wine warehouses had survived in this area, but it prompted the architects to incorporate it in their design, together with other evocative features such as old wine barrels, fragments of old paving, and rails. Completing this trilogy and thematically based on water is the 'Jardin romantique', its dominant feature being a circular artificial lake with a square central island surmounted by a pavilion. Into this flows the dead straight canal that traverses the park, forms its axis of symmetry, and is flanked by promenades resembling pergolas. Planned as a fourth element was a long observation terrace, eight metres high, which was intended to muffle the noise of the expressway beside the Seine and afford

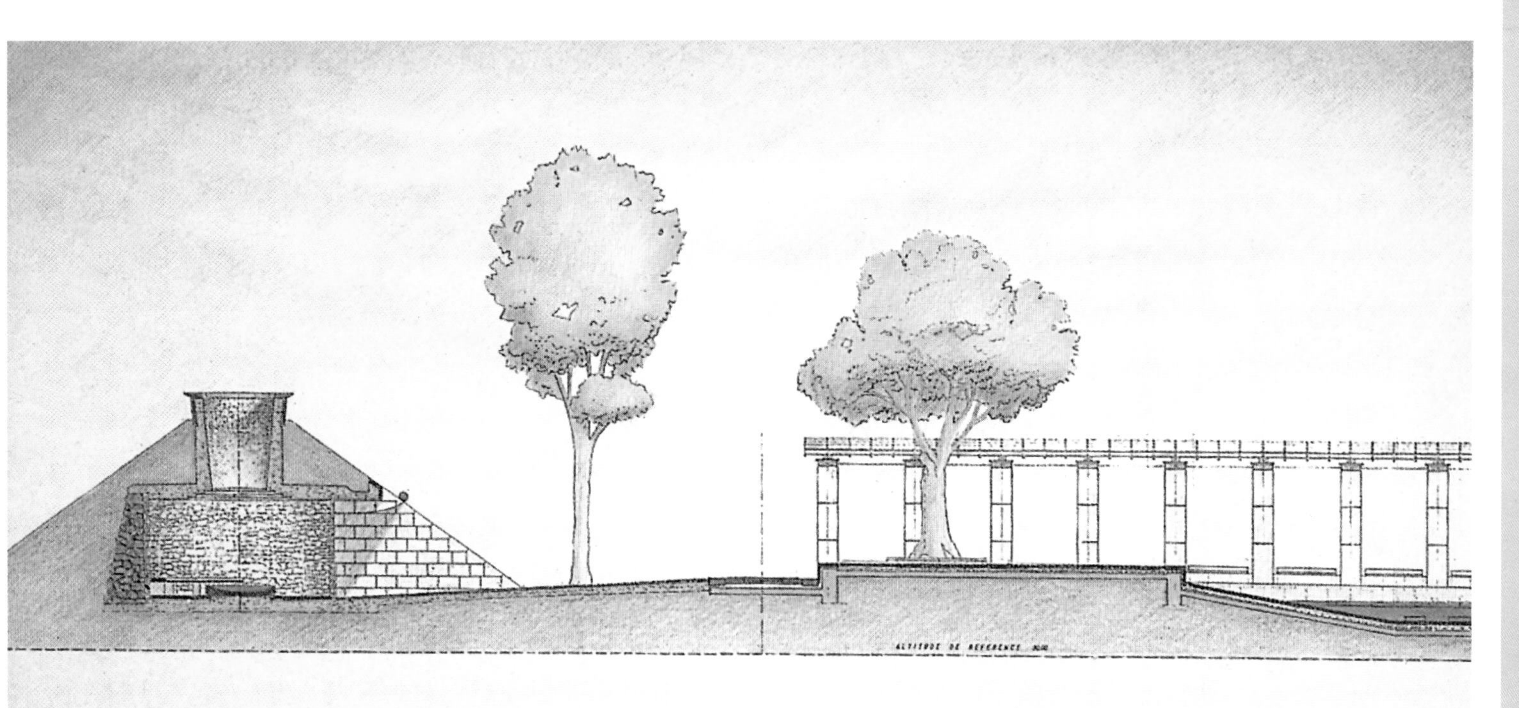

a panoramic view of the urban skyline dominated by the library towers. Originally designed to run the full length of the park in imitation of the Tuileries terraces, this observation platform dwindled, as planning progressed, to a kind of balcony jutting somewhat abruptly above the level of the park on the Seine side. It was not the only sacrifice the architects had to make in order to complete their project with diminished funds. Not as lavishly financed as the designers of the Parc André Citroën, which was completed not long before, they had to make a series of creative sacrifices gravely detrimental to their vision of 'Jardins de la mémoire'. One was the wholesale demolition of the little old wine stores, only one of which has survived in the form of a refurbished relic. They were also obliged to dispense with the greenhouse, that had been intended to form a transparent companion-piece to set against the formal eruptions of Frank O. Gehry's American Center. What also remains is a series of strict architectural accents whose statuesque geometry forms a contrapuntal accompaniment to the organic diversity of the vegetation.
A.G.

The strict architectural accents – like the pavilion – form a contrapuntal accompaniment to the organic diversity of the vegetation.

The clear-cut geometrical structure divides the park into three squares of equal size. Each of these squares is subdivided into nine smaller quadrangles. A dead-straight canal traverses the park; it is bridged by the Rue Dijon before it flows into the circular lake.

The interior of the only surviving wine store, which serves as a reminder of Bercy's former role as one of Paris's largest wine depots. In the future this will function as an exhibition space.

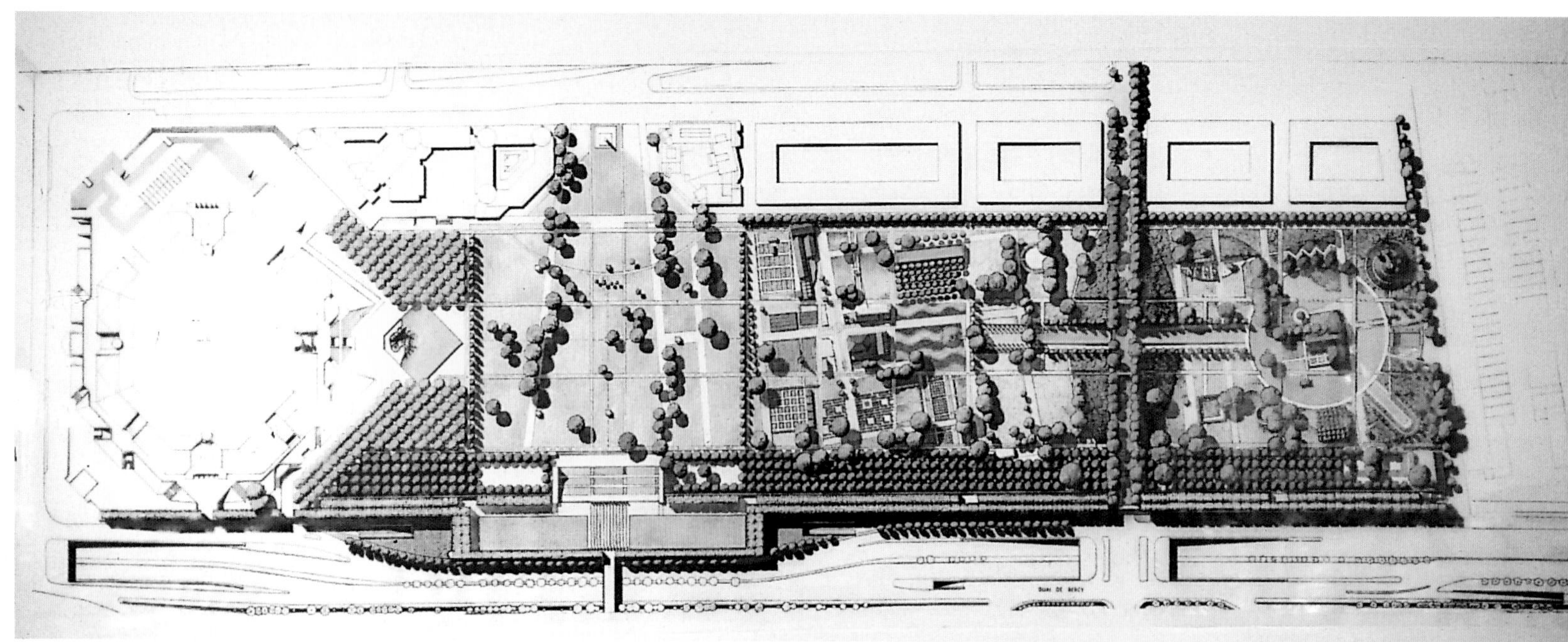

The straight, artificial canal that traverses the park is flanked by promenades resembling pergolas.

In the three squares of the park, the many paved alleys are crossed by the orthogonal grid of the new paths, reconstructing the grid of historic streets.

The north side of the park is flanked by Frank O. Gehry's American Center and an adjacent housing development of rather solid and unspectacular design. In scale and arrangement, these new buildings have eliminated the picturesque complexity of the former wine quarter.

Charlety Stadium and Sports Centre

Henri and Bruno Gaudin

Completion 1994

Visitors are greeted in the entrance hall by an elderly gentleman. He receives them in a rather casual manner, to wit, with his hands in his pockets. A deliberate insult? They are, after all, in Paris's stern Valhalla of physical education, the Stade Charlety. This vast stadium and sports centre, completed in 1994 to designs by the Parisian architects Henri and Bruno Gaudin (father and son), should surely be pervaded by an atmosphere of athletic dynamism, for this is where goals are kicked and aces served, where athletes run faster, jump higher, and throw further. One is all the more surprised by the small plaque that identifies the elderly gentleman – cast life-size in bronze – as Pierre de Coubertin, the father of the modern Olympic Games. It may be that the serenity emanating from the statue in the entrance is intended to convey, in visual terms, the famous French pedagogue and historian's basic philosophy: that feats of athleticism are only a means to an end. Peak performances count for less than fair play and sportsmanship – and, ultimately, publicity. The Olympic idea prescribes that participation is the most important thing.

This idea occurs to the visitor quite naturally at the sight of the sports complex that has urbanistically and architecturally upgraded its surrounding district in the 13th Arrondissement. Why? Because the buildings provide for publicity by their sensitive siting and 'openness' to the city and its life, and because, despite their vast extent on an eight-hectare site (80,000 square metres, no less), they not only dominate that site but treat it in a positively conciliatory manner. The skilful interplay of the variously shaped structures call to mind an urban public space, not an introverted and élitist 'palace of sport' – outwardly, at least. And even there, within the public space, the same principle applies: being there is all that matters.

Visible from afar, four steel lighting masts kindle a desire to participate. They mark the spot and, like gigantic sceptres, dominate the sky above Paris at the point where two brutal saw-blades (the Boulevard Périphérique and, parallel to it, the Boulevard Kellermann) slice a narrow strip off the urban ground-plan south of the Parc de Montsouris. This created an architecturally intractable wasteland that has been restored to urban as well as athletic life by the stadium architecture.

Approaching the complex from the city, one is surprised at the discreet way in which the oval stadium, with its 20,000 covered seats, nestles amid its surroundings. Sunk deep into the ground, the interior can be viewed from skilfully selected angles. Moreover, the open space left between the stadium and the sharp-edged, carefully structured administration block is endowed with an inviting appearance by the steps leading up to the main stand and down into the depths.

Also accessible from the forecourt that cleverly mediates between the stadium, administration block and entrance area is a large hall seating 1400 spectators. This hall sits like a hip joint 'twixt torso and limb, between the stadium and the range of office buildings. In front of it, housed in the bow of a building reminiscent of a ship's towering hull, is the headquarters of the French Olympic Committee. To the south, screened by the stadium's big oval, the hall and the administration block, are eight tennis courts (four of them covered) and a training field encircled by a running track. The architects' principal aim was to deal dialectically with the paradox of a public building 'with a void at its heart' (the sports ground itself): to contrast empty spaces with bulky volumes, confront the static with the mobile, and divorce public (sport) from private (offices).

They succeed primarily in the urban context, but also where the technological aesthetic of the roof structure renders life in the arena transparent in all its power and dynamism. As for the administrative offices where the top brass of the sports bureaucracy 'train' – architectonically speaking – amid massive blocks of natural stone or compete with steel and glass, the architects might have forgone their architectonic strong-man act and consistently 'athletic' styling and adopted a more relaxed approach. Or, better still, have kept their hands in their pockets!

G.M.

Charlety Stadium and Sports Centre

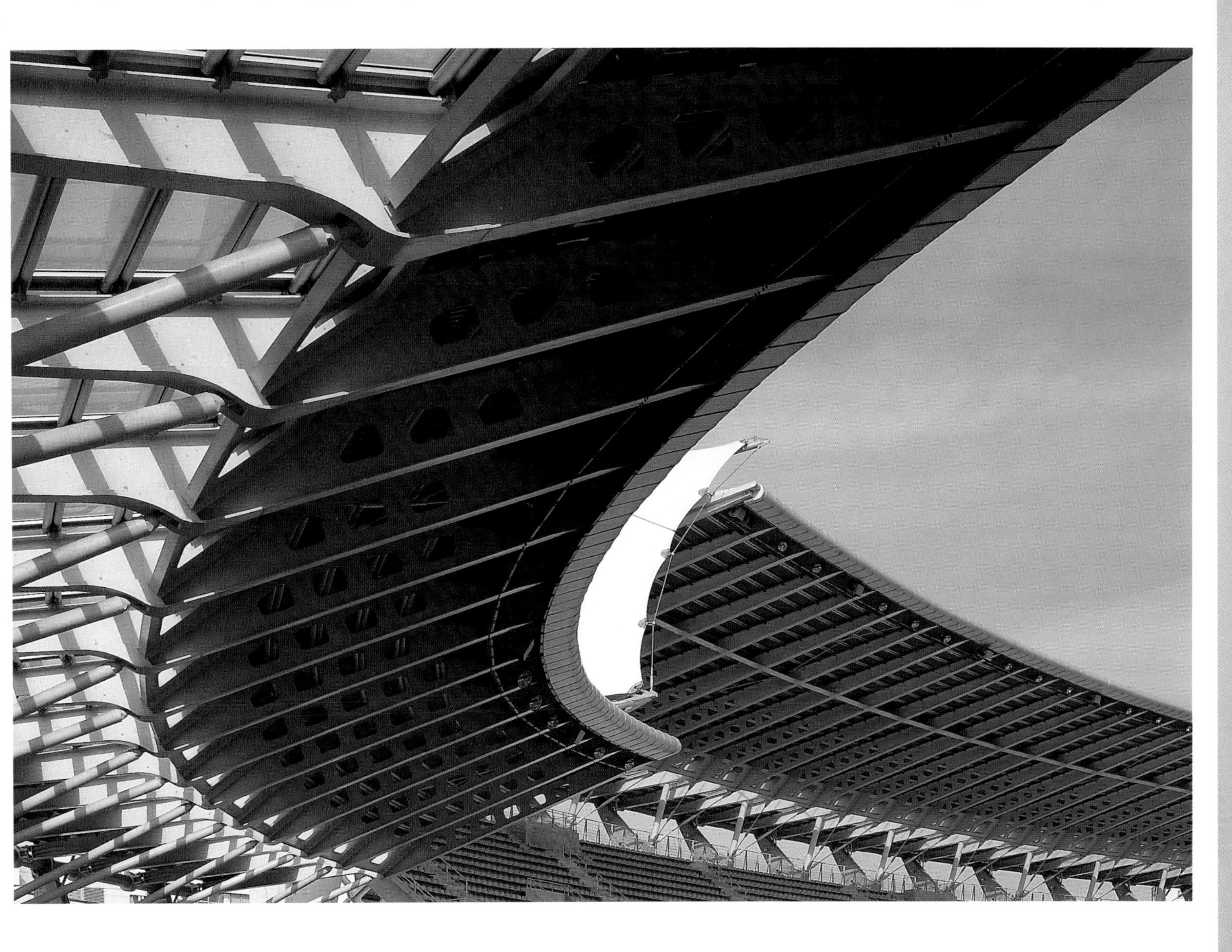

Even the stadium's distinctive
roof construction conveys
a sporting dynamism.
80,000 square metres of
sports architecture have
turned this site in the
13th Arrondissement into
an important attraction.

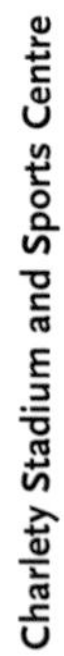

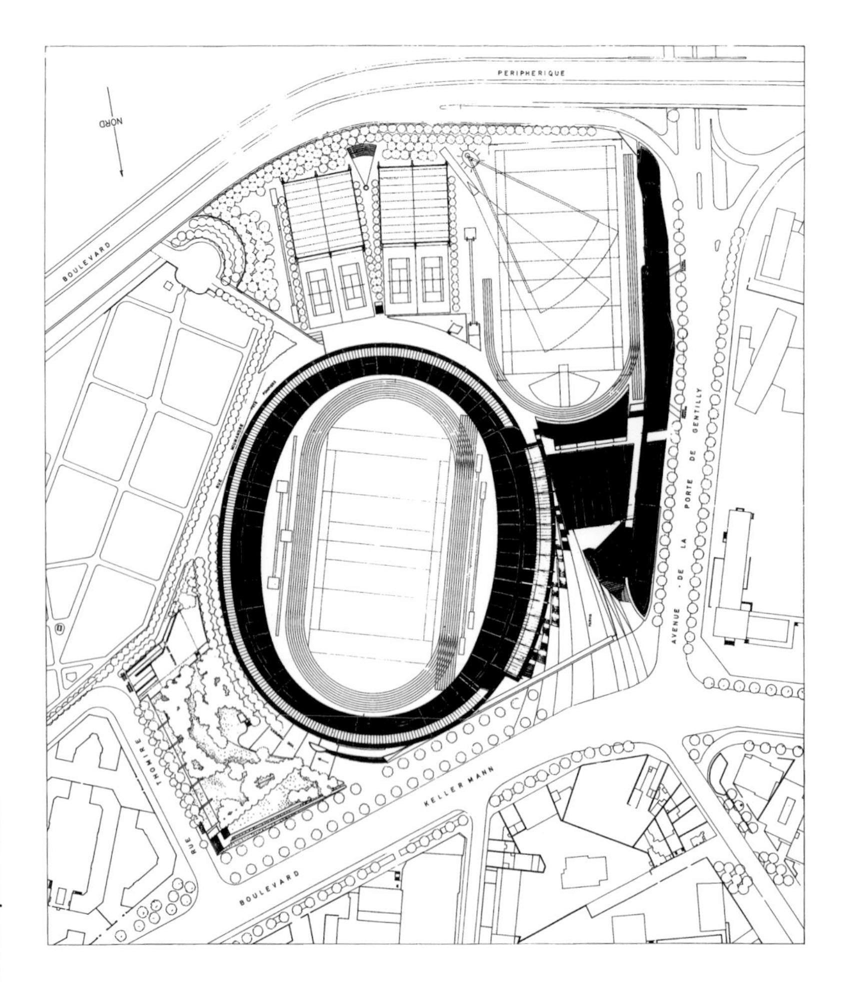

The oval stadium can accommodate a crowd of 20,000, all seats being under cover. Apart from the stadium which appears like an island in the middle of an area badly intersected by major roads, the headquarters of the French Olympic Committee is housed in a long, drawn-out building. Between the two there is a large hall seating 1400 spectators.

Because the stadium
is partially sunken and, from
many angles, the inside
becomes visible from without,
the stadium seems both to
protect and to be inviting
at the same time thanks to
its transparency.

Sporting ambitions not just on the grass:
The statics and design also flex their muscles.
The supporting girders penetrate right through the stands and support both the roof and the terraces.

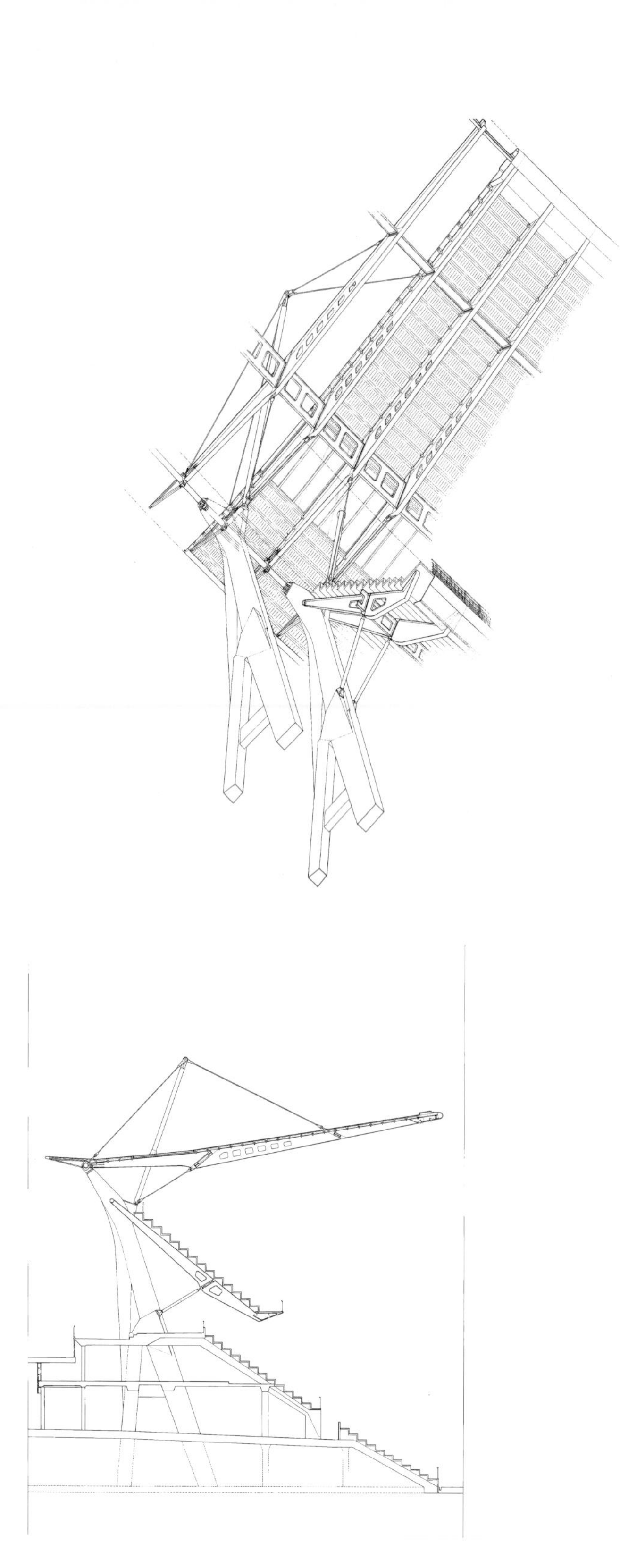

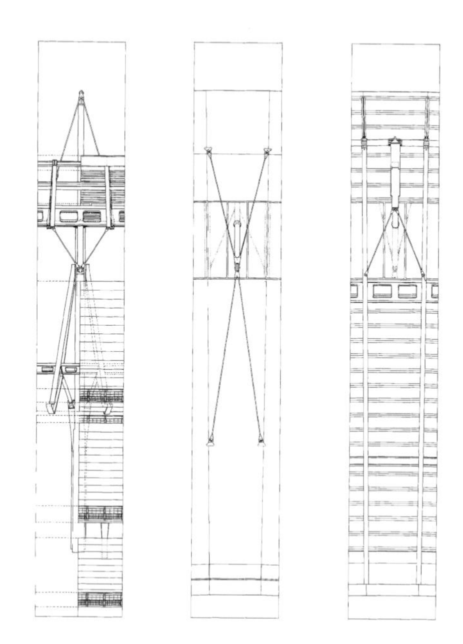

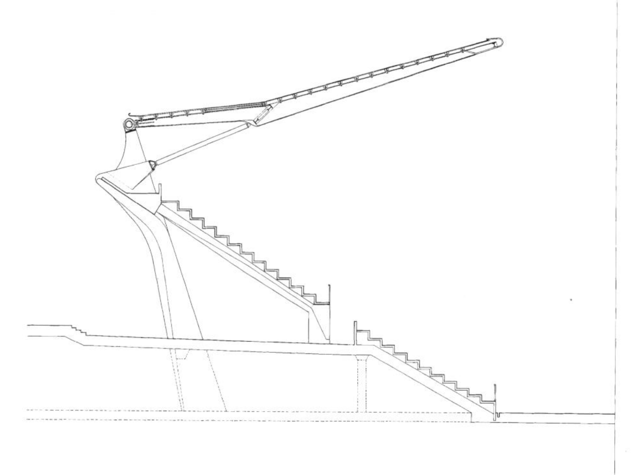

Four steel lighting masts tower over the stadium. The somewhat heavy appearance of the administation block, clad with natural stone slabs (top left), separating the eight tennis courts and trainings arena with running track from the stadium, provides a strong contrast to the dynamic architecture of the main stands.

Grand Stade Paris

Michel Macary, Aymeric Zubléna,
Michel Regembal, Claude Costantini

Completion 1998

Nomen est omen: the name says it all. The Grand Stade at St. Denis is, in fact, France's largest and most ambitious stadium project to date. Erected as the central venue for the World (soccer) Cup of 1998 and additionally conceived with a wistful eye on the Olympics of 2004, this sports arena not only holds 80,000 spectators (more than any other in France) but possesses other record-breaking attributes: access to the stadium is provided by 37 lifts and 18 huge stairways; the roof towers 42 metres above the turf and forms a ring with a surface of 62,000 square metres (4.5 metres thick, the load-bearing members alone weigh 9000 tonnes); 840 workmen and a good million man-hours were required to construct the shell; and the stadium will, by the time it is completed in 1998, have cost over 420 million dollars. What is more, the Grand Stade will also be the biggest monument to which a French premier has ever treated himself, because underlying its soft, pliant, undulating façade is an architectural battle which, after being waged with no holds barred during 1993–4, was eventually decided, arbitrarily and in solitary state, by the then prime minister, Edouard Balladur.

When the decision to build this stadium was taken on 5 October 1994, the curtain came down on an architectural drama staged with passion and cheered and booed throughout the performance. Public opinion in regard to such a major undertaking became polarized from the outset. Because the international football federation (FIFA) had requested the French capital and government to provide the championship with a readily accessible stadium of generous dimensions (and because the economic utilization of such buildings is difficult once a championship is over), a competition was held to find a versatile design of high architectural and urbanistic quality.

The site was quickly found. The Plaine Saint-Denis quarter of Paris is a run-down industrial wasteland situated right beside the motorway and easily reached not only from the two large railway stations in the north (Gare du Nord, Gare de l'Est) but also from Charles de Gaulle Airport: a wilderness perfectly suited to being socially and urbanistically upgraded by the media-effective spectacle of a world football championship. But even urban wastelands sandwiched between ribbons of asphalt and devoid of any recognizable urban pattern are places transformed into neighbourhoods and given identities by human beings. The desert – even the urban desert – is alive. But how can a sports colossus, huge and autistically introverted by nature, communicate with such surroundings, let alone integrate with them? How can its surroundings cope with such a contrast in size? As for the stadium: being built on a world championship scale, how can it ever seem sufficiently homely to the spare-time footballers of the locality?

Though hard enough to master from the architectural aspect alone, these problems were compounded by the promised competition. This was because, with the profitability of the venture in the forefront of their considerations, the authorities restricted entry to investment syndicates, in other words, to groups comprising architects, building contractors and project managers of their own – a dubious limitation. Even the French architects' association expressed misgivings, but they went unheeded. Architects such as Dominique Perrault and the Pritzker Prize-winner Christian de Portzamparc were invited to participate but promptly declined. Of the eighteen teams initially in the running, the only ones left in the final round were the Jean Nouvel group and the Macary-Zubléna, Regembal-Costantini foursome, hitherto known only to insiders. The jury's verdict was unequivocally in favour of Jean Nouvel and his urbanistically cautious and integrative-looking design for a versatile, multifunctional sports centre, 'a city within the city'. The premier's attitude was just as unequivocal: he repudiated the jury and arbitrarily overrode the experts by plumping for the more obviously spectacular solution. Uproar resulted, but building got under way.

Can good architecture come into being under such auspices? We shall not know for sure until 1998. Only then will

On completion, the Grand Stade at St. Denis will be France's largsest sports arena, holding 80,000 spectators. The World (soccer) Cup, 1998 will be staged here.

it be possible to examine the reality of what plans and models can only promise: a sports arena of sensational and possibly handsome appearance but unquestionably introverted character. Will the gigantic open stairways disposed around it like sculptures tempt people to gather there in the 'public space' once the media event is over? Will 'Mexican waves' surge through the huge stands when the masses are applauding other championships elsewhere? Or will the moat that yawns between the stadium and its environs – so theatrically that it looks as if an extraterrestrial space ship has landed there purely by chance – prove too deep? Will the stadium prove too much for the normality of this urban wasteland? Will it prove unusable on the very morrow of the final? If so, it will be more of a memorial than a monument.
G.M.

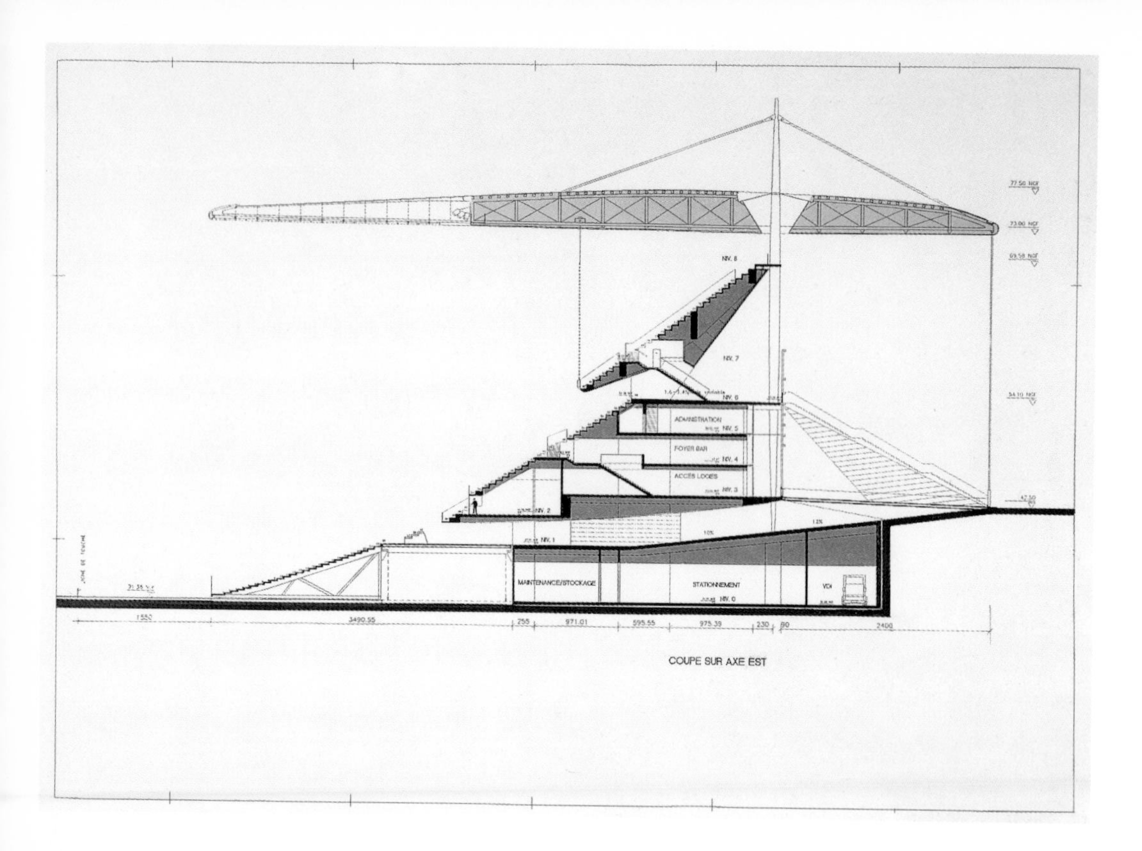

In the run-down industrial wasteland right beside the motorway, this sports colussus of vast proportions threatened to become an autistic urban structure. The roof alone, 42 metres above the grass, forms an oval with a surface area of 62,000 square metres. The complex structural supports weigh 9000 tonnes.

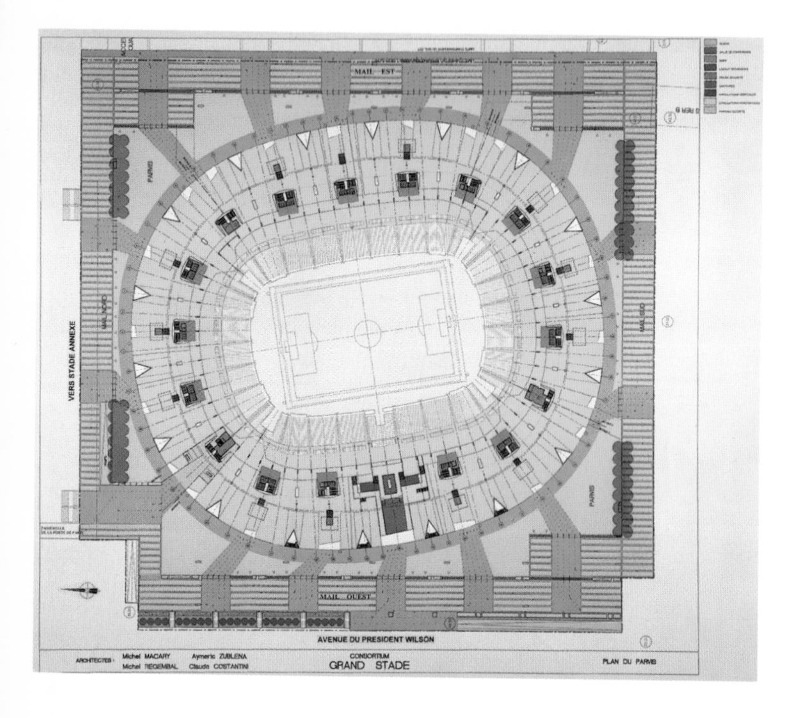

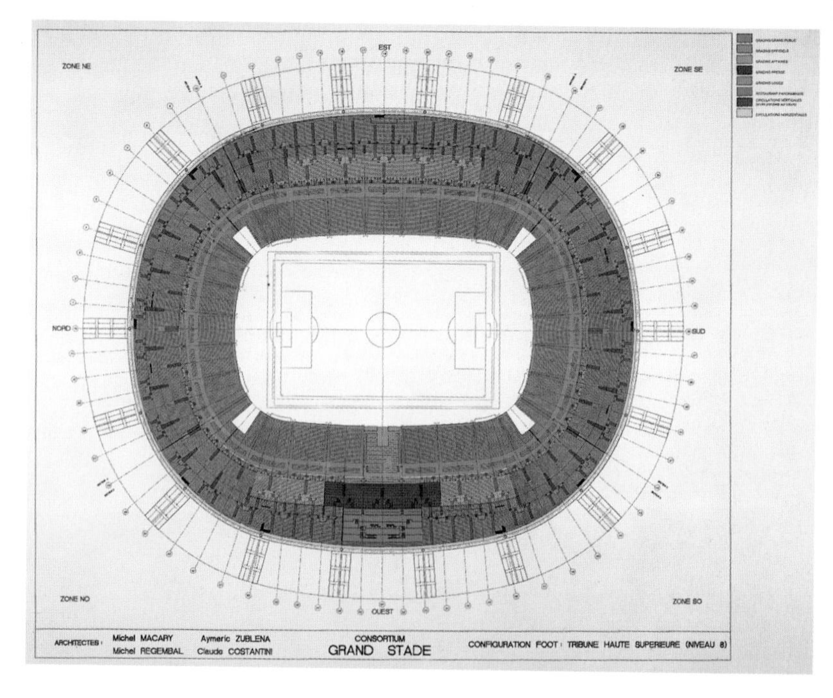

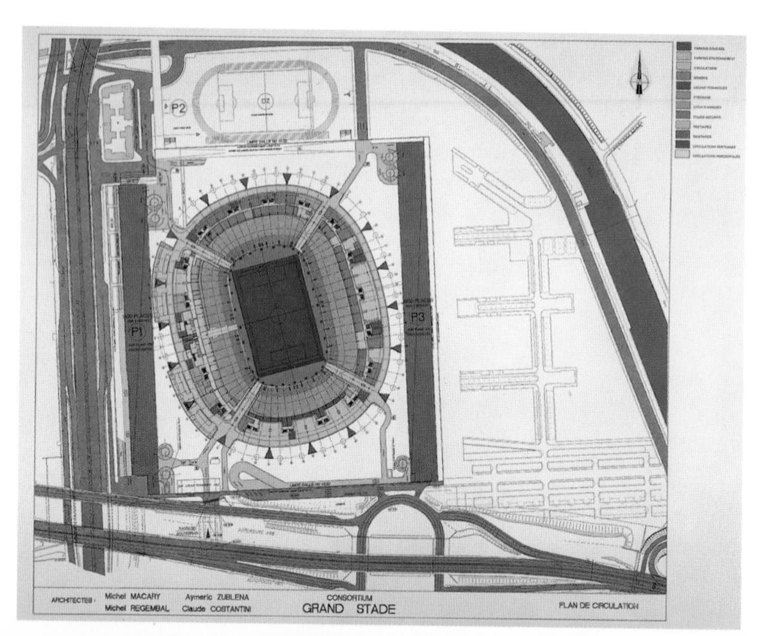

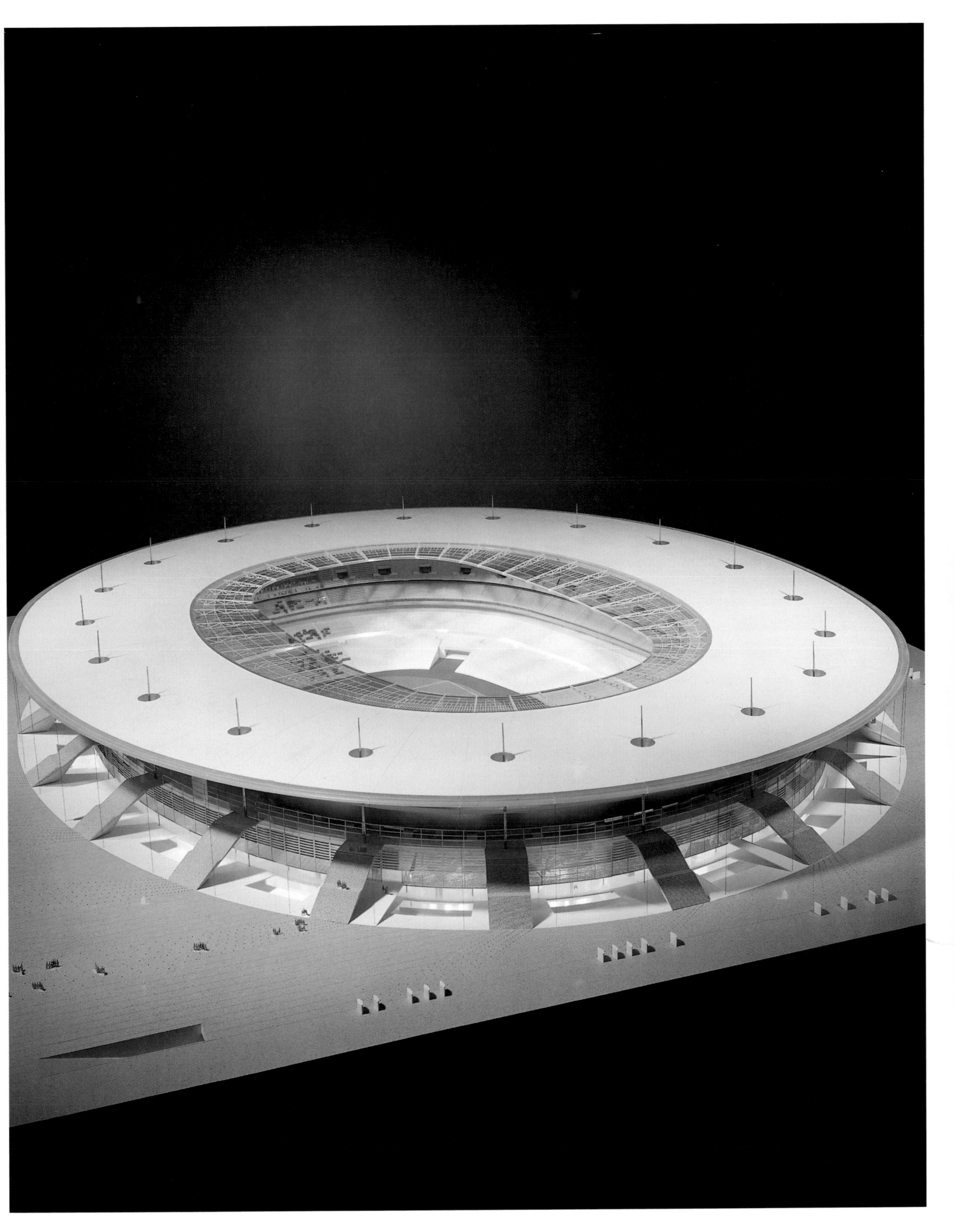

Subsidized Housing Development in Rue Léon-Maurice Nordmann

Patrick Chavannes

Completion 1993

The long, narrow plot in Rue Léon-Maurice Nordmann, a quiet little street in the 13th Arrondissement bounded by Boulevard Arago and the stout walls of the Prison de la Santé, is barely 800 square metres in extent. This is primarily a residential street whose inhabitants live behind inconspicuous façades that range from the two-storeyed reminiscence of a small Art Déco villa, to the somewhat sombre dignity of a residential complex dating from the 1930s, to an eleven-storey high-rise block whose dismal, pitted façade conceals the unloved home of a subsidized housing development of the 1960s. The building line is sporadically interrupted by gateways and courtyards – agreeable extensions of the narrow roadway presenting unexpected views of overgrown gardens and picturesque back yards. Being situated at the point where Rue Léon-Maurice Nordmann describes a gentle curve, Patrick Chavannes's new housing development forms the visual focus of the entire street when seen from the east.

Chavannes paid heed to the heterogeneous nature of the immediate surroundings and, with the architectonic clarity and formal intransigence characteristic of him, embodied it in the spatial disposition of his design. Instead of obtruding on the building line in a solid mass, this falls into three parts of which each contains a varied selection of the total of eighteen apartments. The complex extends to the rear of the plot and occupies its western half. By adopting this conformation, it not only responds to the differing heights and abrupt transitions of the neighbouring buildings but presents, on a very restricted site, a miniature typology of inner-city living accommodation. The entrance to the underground garage is surmounted by a four-storeyed structure, only one room wide, which conforms to the buildings in the west, whereas the adjoining ten-storey tower is almost as high as the 1960s high-rise block beyond it and mercifully conceals the latter's fire wall. This tower inserts an architectural punctuation mark and dramatizes the view of the street. Set at an angle to the main axis and relieved by large windows, the façade catches the morning sunlight, which is broken up and hatched with shadows by horizontal brise-soleils. The siting of the tower provides a transition to the courtyard area, which occupies the eastern half of the site and wrests some space – albeit only visual space apparent to the chance passer-by – from the cramped confines of an inner-city (subsidized) housing development.

Looking through the railings, which are there partly as a protection from vandalism, a kind of garden courtyard can be seen. The spatial versatility of this area serves a dual purpose: to enable the curious passer-by to explore the inner life of a Parisian courtyard, and to preserve the residents' intimacy and privacy. Adjoining this is the rearward block, whose three eastward-facing, fully glazed storeys surmount a base consisting of maisonettes. The 'base' – and this contributes to the garden courtyard's skilful use of space – is set in a terraced area spanned by slender steel footbridges whose plank decks lead to the maisonettes' entrances. The six single-storey apartments above them are accessible from the side: by way of an open staircase in the north and the tower lift in the south.

And this brings us to a subject especially dear to the architect's heart: his aim was to provide each apartment with an individual, 'dignified' access rather than waste scarce space by inserting voluminous passages and staircases. Supplemented by lifts, the covered walkways and external stairways and, more especially, the steel footbridges which Chavannes had used in 1988 for his studio apartments in Rue de la Prairie are a major design element that enhances their spatial vitality and formal variety. Not just externally, either, for where they are connected to maisonettes and triplexes, in particular, the standardized dimensions of these dwellings acquire greater spatial individuality and autonomy. Moreover, Chavannes' apartment house for young post office staff in Rue de Daumesnil shows how stairs inside apartments can become a structural element that affects the texture of the façade. There, unusually enough, the street side is entirely glazed, affording unrestricted views of the apartments' interiors and, conversely, a view of the busy street from within. Painted white, the banisters of the internal stairs stand out against the transparent façade. In conjunction with the permanently installed, room-high roller blinds whose design was an independent artistic process (in this case, the computer-alienated Marianne on France's postage stamps), they create a rhythmical structure

Crossing a sunken terraced area, slender steel footbridges with plank decks lead to the entrances of maisonettes in the rearward block.

that endows an apparently mundane and functionalistic façade with subtle aesthetic tension.

In Rue Nordmann, Chavannes has used sliding wooden panels in luminous red and vivid blue instead of roller blinds. Mounted only a few feet behind the delicate framework of the conservatory-style glazing, they form a second, mobile partition capable of varying the otherwise white and grey expanses of wall in an exciting way and – a not unimportant consideration – of restoring the requisite privacy. The architecture here is particularly open and transparent on the courtyard side, where terracing, footbridges and a dense thicket of bamboo successfully create a spatial complexity productive of an interrelationship between private and communal areas which the residents clearly appreciate. The clumps of bamboo and the courtyard's plank floor complete a spectrum of material effects that reconciles glass and paintwork with plaster and the close mesh metal sheets that encase the north side of the tower, effortlessly harmonizing concrete with steel and timber.

A.G.

Coming from an easterly direction along the slight bend in Rue Léon-Maurice Nordmann, the tower block, set at an angle to the line of the other buildings, automatically attracts attention. The generously large windows allow the morning sun to flood the 3 roomed flats. A grid of horizontal sun blinds casts dark shadows across the façade, providing a subtle contrast to the neighbouring wall surfaces which are clad with holed metal sheets.

The three-storey façade to the courtyard is completed glazed and looks like a huge wintergarden. Immediately behind the window grid, the architect has included sliding wall panels, painted brilliant red and deep blue. This second, moving layer in an otherwise white and grey façade, adds an exciting element of variety as well as providing some discretion.

Plans and elevations.
Underground parking on three levels solves the car problem, leaving room for a terraced garden and a small internal courtyard for everybody to use.

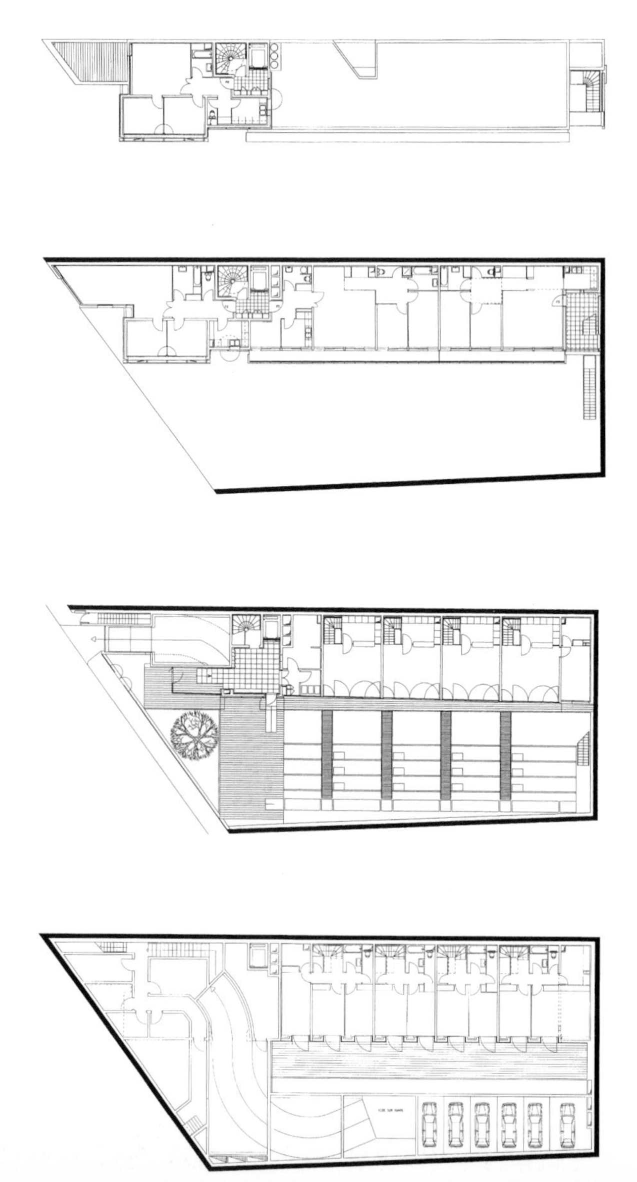

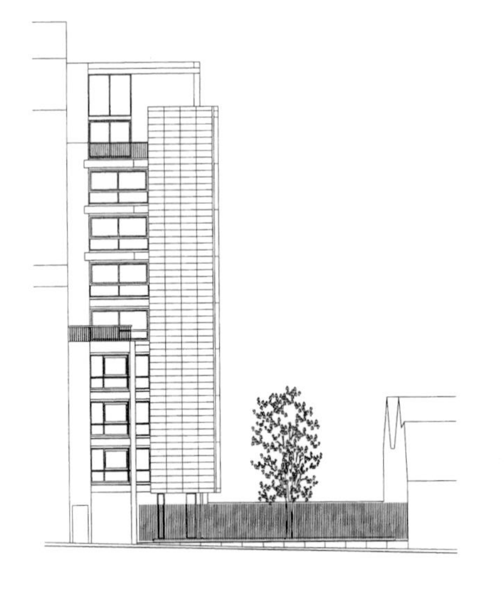

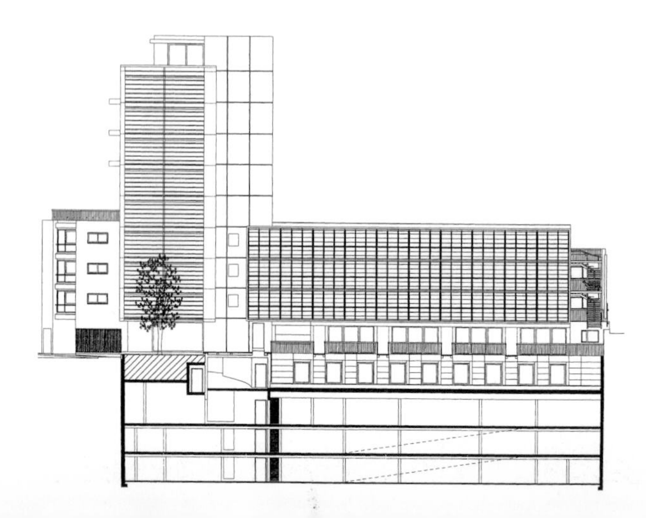

Apartment House in Rue de Bellièvre

Fabrice Dusapin, François Leclercq

Completion 1987

'Isn't Paris a noble ship?' demanded Honoré de Balzac in 1834, on one of his literary excursions through the French capital. And indeed, the city's germ-cell reposes like a pebble in the middle of the Seine, for its urban conformation derives from the crossing-point where, in prehistoric times, the two plateau spurs of Montmartre and Belleville were connected by a route that straddled the two islands now known as the Ile de la Cité and the Ile de St.-Louis. Now, 162 years after Balzac penned his proud rhetorical question, the romantic and touristically profitable image of 'the city on the Seine' is coloured by its famous bridges, its riverside promenades, its pleasure-boats equipped with powerful floodlights, and its old barges converted into picturesque houseboats. But Paris – and this is less well known – is also France's largest inland port; and where commerce is concerned, there the 'nobility' invoked by Balzac sometimes loses its aura. This is certainly so where the city develops south-westwards into the immense, unromantic dockland that sprawls along the river beyond the Gare d'Austerlitz – where promenades yield to motorways and river barges to gross registered tonnes. It is in this rather inhospitable but nonetheless lively neighbourhood that the new Ministry of Finance has 'docked' with its massive bulk jutting riverwards.

It was proposed some ten years ago to create inexpensive living accommodation for (unmarried) 'crew members' of this brutish bureaucratic vessel. The authorities hit upon a Left Bank site in Rue de Bellièvre, just across the river. Given that the quarter is now being massively upgraded by residential and office developments, and that the skilful architecture of Dominique Perrault's Bibliothèque Nationale François Mitterrand (see p. 42) is proving an added attraction, to call it a 'dockland' may soon be anachronistic. However, it was still a desolate area when the Parisian architects Fabrice Dusapin and François Leclercq, faced with the need to fit 44 'studios', or one-room, apartments into a gap between a youth hostel and a relic of the 1870s, designed a thoroughly elegant building sheathed in brilliant white.

In so doing they countered its surroundings and quoted from them in equal measure. On the street side, their building skilfully mediates between its tall, projecting neighbours by interposing two cubes of varied conformation. With its austere covered access pathways and delicate, overhanging roofs, its transparent transitions that link the two halves in a manner reminiscent of ship's bridges, and even its curiously massive spiral stairway, that somehow seems to float accentuating the building's verticals in contrast to its predominantly horizontal structure, it looks like a quotation from the classical Moderne and its 'ocean liner' style. This is a ship, but a stranded one. Stranded because the luminous elegance of its fabric is already, after only nine years, succumbing to the darkness of decay. The once smooth and flawless façade is threaded with cracks, crevices and varicose veins. The windows of the studio apartments, which were frugally appointed like the identical cells in a honeycomb (with small prefabricated shower rooms and one short row of cupboards and kitchen appliances, and a rectangular living-room), are thick with dust. The wooden doors have swollen and, in some cases, become structurally unhinged. Metal components are rusting and reinforcing rods are showing through the concrete in places. The surroundings are neglected. Only occasionally do the few remaining residents of this semi-derelict housing development strive to mitigate the desolation of the covered ways by adorning them with thirsty cacti and desiccated palms.

It is a shame about this building. Its architecture is far from frivolous; on the contrary, it fits discreetly into the unedifying environs of the Quai d'Austerlitz. The continuous base area skilfully connects the two differing volumes, whose stratification is immediately apparent to the eye. The gap between the cubes creates interesting perspectives,

Not far from the Ministry of Finance on the banks of the Seine in the 13th Arrondissement, is a building which provides inexpensive living accommodation for "unmarried members of staff". The complex with its 44 one-room studio apartments stands out from all the other buildings in this dockland area and yet fits in perfectly.

looks eloquent and inviting. Then there is the frontage's subtle interplay of form and material: flush-fitted, aluminium-framed windows, Carrara marble, glazed slits, a stairway that communicates with the street and spirals upwards from the forecourt. All these things constitute excellent and attractive architecture. Or are they just aestheticism, and, for that very reason, manifestly unpopular in such a socially sensitive district? Is the architecture too stagey? Does it display too many refinements incapable of taking root in a rather rough-and-ready neighbourhood? Paris may not, after all, be a 'noble ship' throughout its length and breadth. Nor a luxury liner – not, at any rate, where the only berths are in steerage.

G.M.

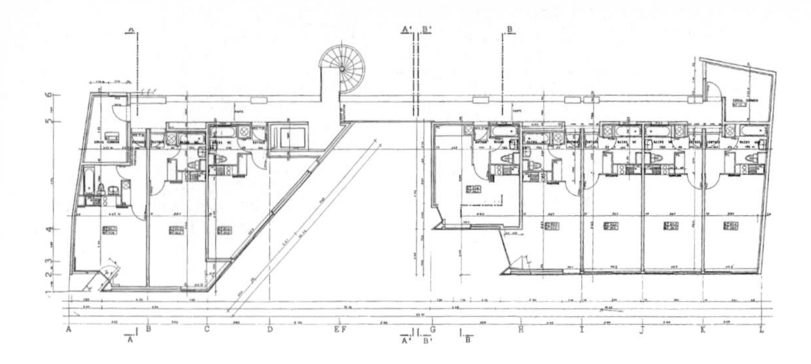

Two sections of the building of differing height are connected by the forecourt, the spiral stairs and the covered ways to form one strictly regimented ensemble. The layered, elegantly proportioned façades, with their rows of aluminium windows are linked together by the massive base under the whole complex.

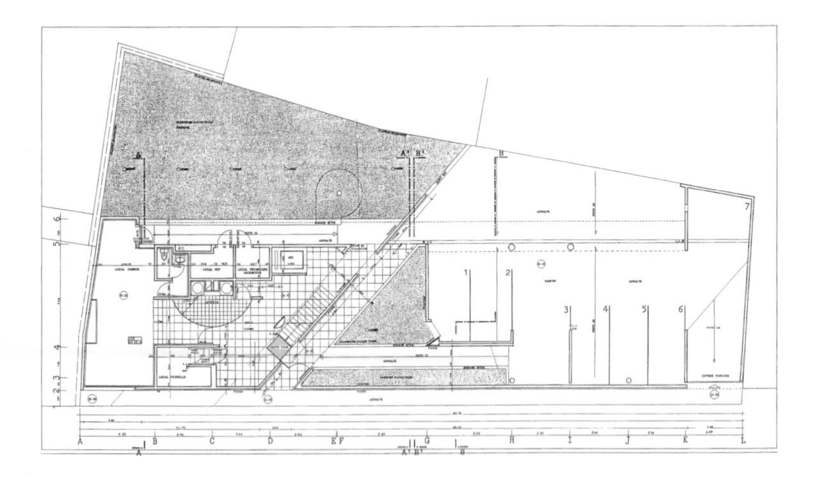

Apartment House in Rue de l'Ourcq

Philippe Gazeau

Completion 1994

Rue de l'Ourcq....
The name means little even to ardent architect(ourist)s and connoisseurs of Paris. A small street north-east of the Gare du Nord, it winds through the 19th Arrondissement as unassumingly as if it were afraid of the thunderous and far bigger Boulevard Périphérique, the urban motorway and its metal serpent that holds the city fast like an antediluvian reptile come to life in the modern age of mobility. The neighbourhood to which the street gives access is not a handsome one, though it does still display modest but pleasantly proportioned buildings whose characteristic chimney-pots seem to greet one from an intricate roof-top landscape – buildings which arose on those plots that so fortunately became available when land in the old 19th-century suburbs was divided up into smaller parcels.

But another form of greeting is perceptible here: 'Bonjour tristesse!' Undulating throughout the quarter are those outsize, bloated worms of apartment houses that wriggled off drawing-boards everywhere during the 1970s, as pallid in terms of architectural expression as the once garish colours that cloaked these faceless residential fortresses have since become. Lovers of architecture will be disinclined to linger in Rue de l'Ourcq for another reason: the alluring proximity of the Parc de la Villette, with its architectural spectacles and extravaganzas (see p. 50). Yet visitors to this same neighbourhood can also marvel at an architectural jewel that aspires to be no more than a straightforward apartment house in present-day garb. And because it fulfils that aim so shrewdly and uncompromisingly, amiably and unobtrusively, it gives evidence, even in its role as a subsidized housing development, of great architecture.

The Parisian architect responsible for this building is Philippe Gazeau, whose professional commitment earned him the 'Prix d'Architecture du Moniteur' in 1994. It was built, and well built, without any striving for effect – but, to quote Gazeau himself, 'with great pleasure in the construction'; without any architectural showbiz – but in an attempt to reveal the building's 'components' and identity and 'render them accessible'; and without ignoring its surroundings – but in a thoroughly 'self-assured and autonomous' manner. An additional contribution to its success was the desire of its sponsors – the post office housing association founded in 1957 and significantly entitled 'Toit et Joie', or 'Roof and Joy', which also initiated the buildings in Rue Oberkampf and Rue Etienne-Dolet (see pp. 104 and 154) – to provide young postal workers with architecturally ambitious living quarters under the auspices of the Paris post office building programme of the late 1980s. As, for instance, in the Rue de l'Ourcq development.

Since 1993, 26 tailor-made apartments have been accommodated in this austere but far from unsightly building, which is set quite a long way back from its neighbours. There is an explanation for this initially puzzling fact: under the provisions of a regrettable but valid building regulation, the street may some day be widened as a belated tribute to the car-friendly French capital.

One consolation is that this setback enabled Gazeau to provide the building with a kind of forecourt used by a ground-floor café possessed of sun umbrellas and a certain robust charm. This is situated beside the entrance to the underground garage, which boasts 31 (!) parking spaces. Seen from here, the building immediately discloses its architectural response to the narrow site: three segments govern the language of the façade and the available space. Two of these comprise five accommodation levels each. Set back above them on the sixth floor, a maisonette with a small terrace forms the building's upper extremity. Running between these two solid blocks is a very light, transparent 'access passage'. Therein lies the true secret and architec-

Two narrow sections fill the gap in the 19th Arrondissement. Between them there is a generously proportioned entrance passage with boarded wooden floors. From here, superb vistas across the Parisian cityscape can be enjoyed.

tural beauty of this simple building: it is a celebration of space. The open access levels – a steel framework which, with floorboards of fine woods, makes the visitor feel he should remove his shoes in summer – are linked by outside stairways. The forecourt, with its free composition of standing and recumbent cubes flanked by rough, undressed fire walls, its third range of buildings and stretch of grass at the rear, is a cleverly devised and finely balanced landscape that lends intimacy to the residential world around the 'passage'. The building's massive horizontals make a spacious impression amid its verticals. This is because, with their carefully equilibrated interplay of volumes and planes on the courtyard side, they facilitate lively communion and peaceful privacy in equal measure, thereby giving evidence of architectural distinction in the midst of a depressing neighbourhood. Bonjour noblesse!

G.M.

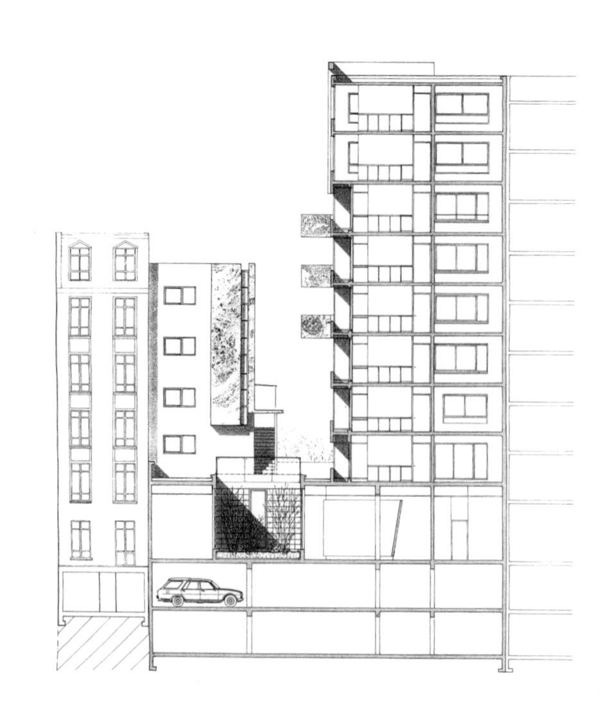

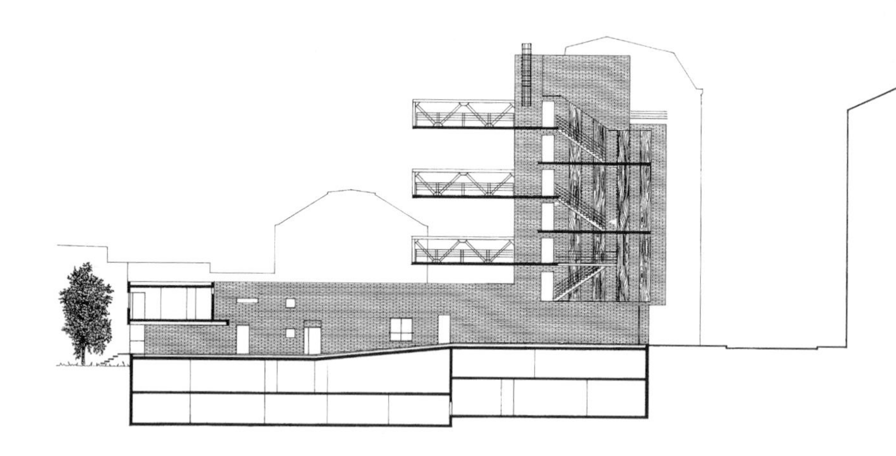

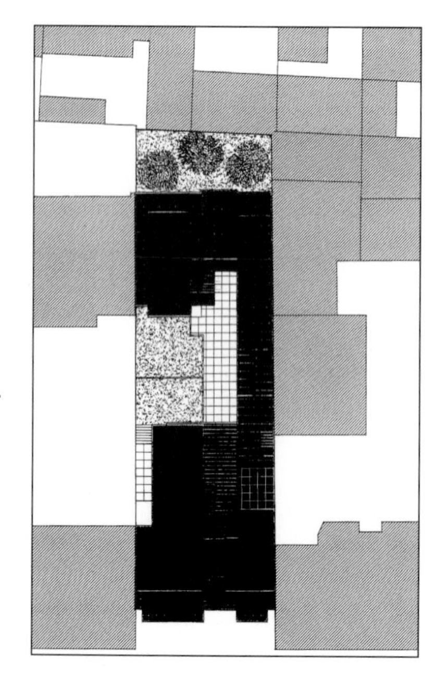

The imposing balconies open into the apartments. A massive steel framework was designed to support the projecting structures.

On warm days, the balconies are jointly used.

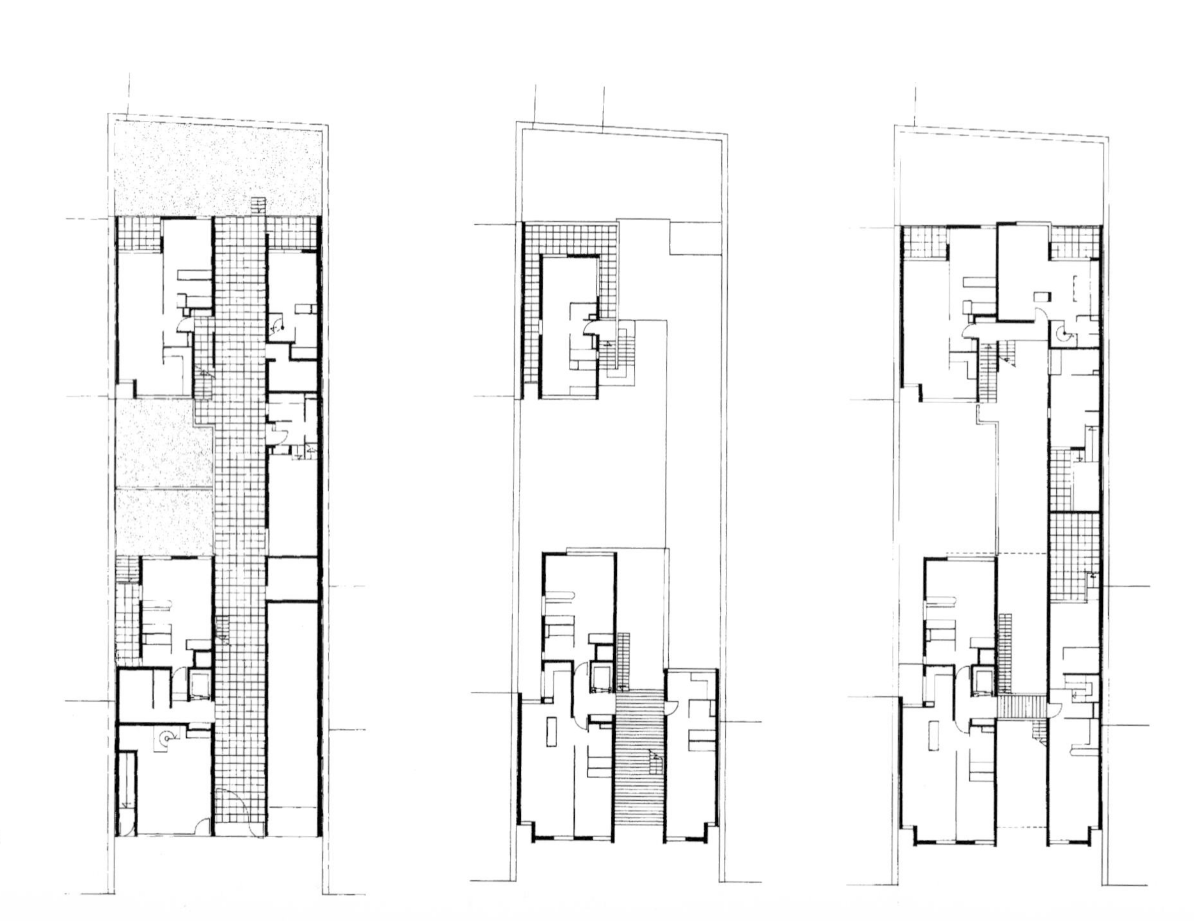

Interior view of a maisonette apartment.

Apartment House with Integrated Post Office in Rue Etienne-Dolet

Olivier Brénac, Xavier Gonzalez

Constructed 1991–3

This quarter in the easterly 20th Arrondissement is one of those districts where, remote from the strongholds of tourism and celebrated museums, major cultural centres and luxuriant parks, shopping malls and arterial roads, one can still hear the authentic beat of the French capital's heart: the 'life' of the street – a rare phenomenon in our cities, which, on the threshold of the 3rd millennium, are everywhere mutating into lifeless service centres and anonymous traffic junctions on the data highways. Speech and conversation, exchange and communication are the architects of this urban life. What matters is dialogue – dialogue between places and buildings as well as people.

Since 1993 it has been possible to see an architecture capable of urban dialogue in Rue Etienne-Dolet – indeed, almost to hear it, because the theme of the building in question is the mutual loquacity of its cubes, the communicativeness of its façade, and its place in the context of town planning and architectural history: in short, the narrative power of the architectonic. Designed by the Parisian architects Olivier Brénac and Xavier Gonzalez, it houses 40 apartments and a new post office.

This 'healing' of a gaping wound in the city's fabric – a vacant lot, all of 850 square metres in extent, sandwiched between Rue Etienne-Dolet and Rue des Maronites not far from the church of Notre-Dame-de-la-Croix – was also initiated by the post office building programme. It is apparent that these are post office premises as soon as one stands in front of the glazed corner of the post office as if confronted by a gigantic shop window two storeys high. The interior is distinguished by the severe and dynamic solidity of the continuous, glass-enclosed counter. The exterior displays a concrete framework that lends spatial stability to a small open courtyard in front of the building and cites the original building line. Together with a narrow strip of glass beneath the apartments that begin on the third floor, this serves to mark out the post office visually from the complex of neighbouring volumes, which are are staggered and vary in height.

For that is the true essence of this eloquent architectural narrative: because the building on this lot had to mediate in shape between a tall building of the 1960s set further back, and a much lower, typically Parisian apartment house of the last century, the architects split their building into three blocks grouped at first-floor level around an open courtyard. The tallest of these blocks is set back from the street and conforms in height to its 'modern' eight-storey neighbour. The smaller, jauntier block that projects on the left nestles discreetly against Rue Etienne-Dolet's earlier architecture despite its austere façade of glass, pale stone slabs and black marble, and despite the row of columns that rounds off its roof.

'The missing link in the chain' is what the two architects call this composition of volumes. They wanted the historical legacy of this heterogeneous urban quarter and their building's own, architecturally uncompromising stance in 'the world of today' to engage in a tension-charged dialogue. The interior conveys a similar message, for cubic constraints affected the skilful design of the economically appointed two-room apartments, six of which could be fitted into each storey. They are entered by way of an L-shaped passage, sometimes built around the shower room, or provided with a central forum in the shape of the kitchen. As for what the inner courtyard surmounting the post office achieves, it is this above all: conversational give-and-take, in other words, dialogue. Apartments, communal spaces, façade, adaptation to the existing urban fabric – a building as 'animate' and polyphonous as this fits well into such a neighbourhood.

G.M.

Apartment House in Rue Etienne-Dolet

Near the church Notre-Dame de la Croix: a game with cubes between unforgiving neighbours – namely a typical Parisian turn-of-the-century town house and building from the '60s, three storeys higher.

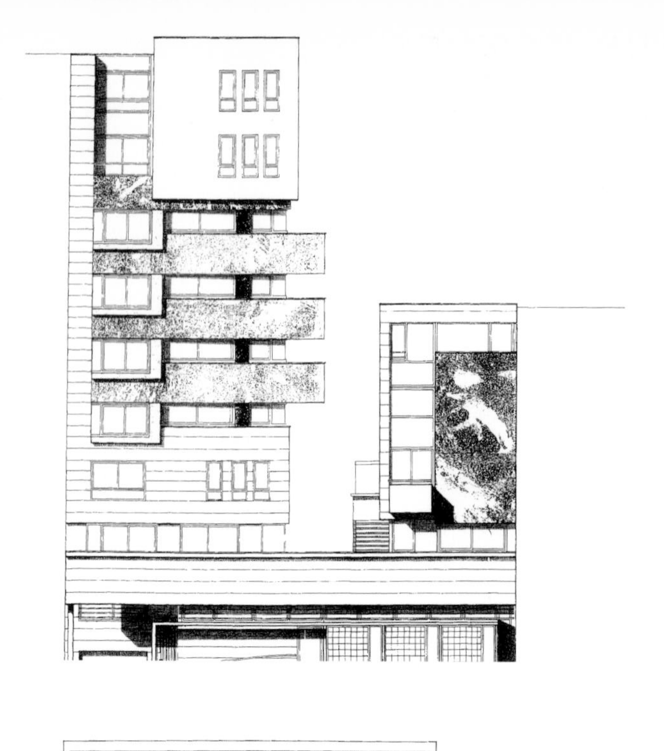

A composition of cubic spaces has been arranged around a courtyard between the Rue Etienne-Dolet and Rue des Maronites which runs parallel. Each storey comprises 6 apartments. The courtyard, which is built on top of the post office, has been given a wooden floor.

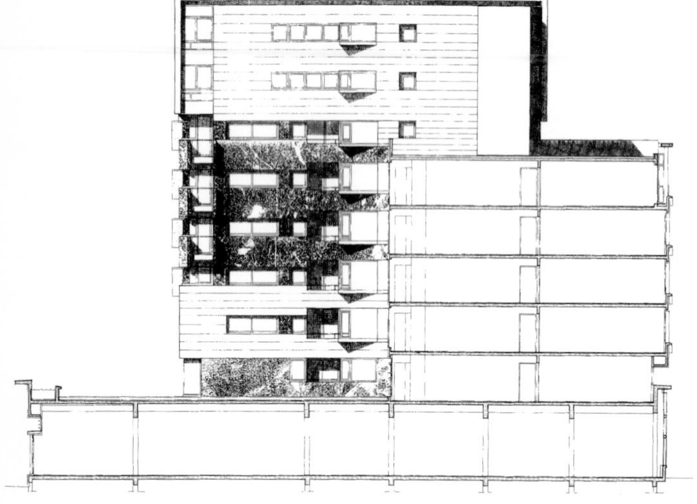

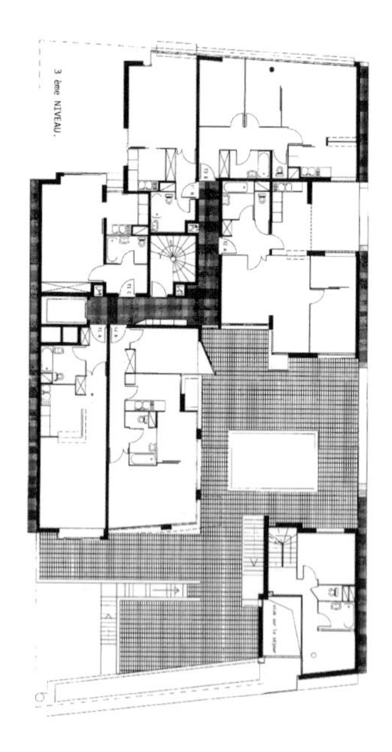

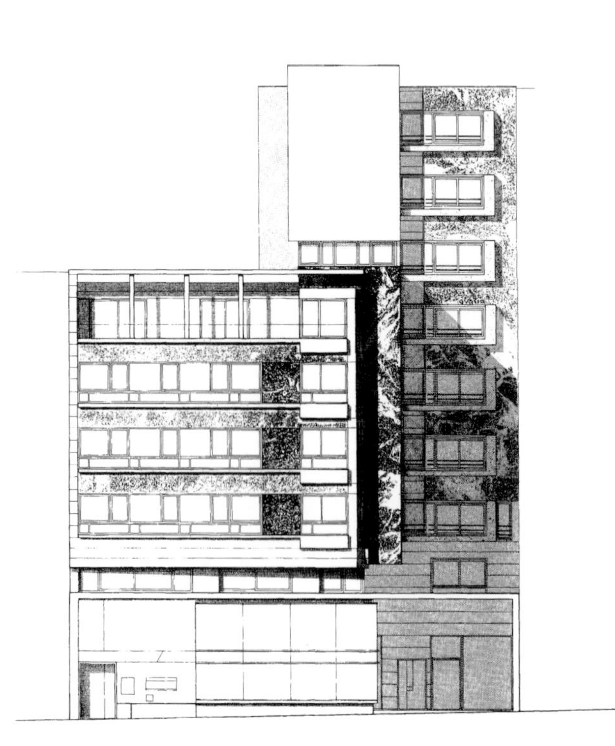

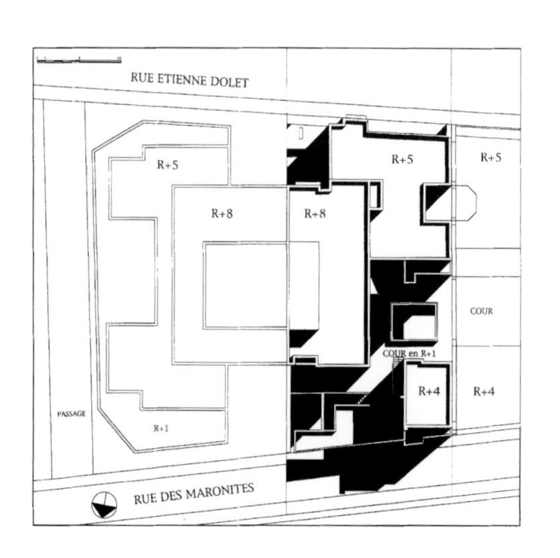

The apartments are small but full of light.
The post office can be reached from the street
via an invitingly designed square.
A large mirror in the post office conceals access to the
technical installations and rooms for members of staff.
All areas in this strictly composed ensemble have
something in common: a well orchestrated play
with shapes, colours and materials.

LA POSTE
Guichet automatique
LA POSTE
Boîtes aux lettres

Photographic credits

Pictorial material was kindly supplied by the respective architectural practices as well as by the following photographers:

Hervé Abbadie 142 top

Raoul Arroche 29

Luc Boegly 36 bottom, 40 top

Nicolas Borel 25, 61 (2 illus.), 63 (2 illus.), 64/65, 66 (2 illus.), 67, 68, 69 (3 illus.), 96 top, 105 top, 107, 109 (3 illus.), 110 bottom, 111 (2 illus.)

J.Y. Cousseau 122 top, center

Stéphane Couturier, Archipress 35 bottom, 40 left, bottom right, 131, 132 top, 133, 135 (3 illus.), 158 (3 illus.), 159

C. Demonfaucon 96 bottom right

EPPV/F.X. Bouchart (Courtesy Mission Interministerielle des Grands Travaux) 58 bottom

Felipe Ferré 31

Georges Fessy, Michel Denancé 47, 48 top/center, 49

Scott Frances, Esto Photographics 90 top, 91

Serge Hambourg 33

Chapon Hervé 14 top

Koji Horiuchi 36 center

Leonard Jacobson 36 top

Raimund Koch 30 top, center

Waltraud Krase 30 left/bottom right, 37, 39, 52 (4 illus.), 53, 58 center, 59 bottom, 99, 101, 102 left/top right, 103 (3 illus.), 123, 125 top

Jean Marie Monthiers 54/55, 58 top, 59 top, 141, 143, 149, 151, 152 top (2 illus.), 155, 157

Patrick Müller 71, 73, 74 (3 illus.), 75

Christian Richters 24, 43, 44 top, 45, 48 bottom, 77, 79, 80 (2 illus.), 81 (2 illus.), 102 bottom

Deidi von Schaewen 41

F.J. Urquijo 124 top, 125 bottom

Hans Werlemann 113, 115